Ben Baxter has written ... challenge pastors to be better informed linguistically and hence to be able to be more responsible exegetes. We who teach and preach the Scriptures are given a tremendous privilege and opportunity to open God's word for our people, and we cannot afford to make serious mistakes that misconstrue its meaning. Although often overlooked, language study stands at the heart of good exegesis. Baxter's book will be a valuable tool to help pastors and teachers avoid falling into some of the common errors and abuses of interpretation of the Bible. I highly recommend that pastors read and, more importantly, learn from and use this book.

Stanley E. Porter, Ph.D.
Professor of New Testament, President and Dean,
McMaster Divinity College
Hamilton, Ontario, Canada

Benjamin Baxter has provided a succinct and accessible guide to analyzing words for biblical exegesis. He not only lays out foundational principles, rooted in linguistics, but then provides case studies in both Hebrew and Greek for those who want to hone their exegetical skills for interpreting the Old and New Testaments. This will help any student of Scripture who wants to avoid the pitfalls of word studies that have plagued biblical exegesis for centuries and discover the meaning of the biblical text holistically.

Mark J. Boda, Ph.D.
Professor of Old Testament, McMaster Divinity College
Professor, Faculty of Theology, McMaster University

"In the Original Text It Says", which can be read in a day, might disguise with its short length the tremendous assistance offered for evaluating with cautious discernment original language word analysis encountered in typical commentaries found in the libraries of busy pastors and Bible teachers. The

book is a genuinely profitable and pragmatic "how to" manual with detailed examples for teaching and preaching using word-study and language-in-context principles that do not require intimate familiarity with original languages, but itself is thoroughly grounded in both Hebrew and Greek. A great resource to help avoid the most common word-study fallacies, yet capitalize on the value of original language material offered in commentaries.

Gerald L. Stevens, Ph.D.
Professor of New Testament and Greek
New Orleans Baptist Theological Seminary

Benjamin J. Baxter has his MA in Christian Studies from McMaster Divinity College in Hamilton, Ontario, Canada, where he wrote his thesis examining and critiquing 32 commentaries from a modern linguistic perspective using two Old Testament and two New Testament passage. He has previously published two articles dealing with Biblical words and word studies for the *McMaster Journal of Theology and Ministry. "In the Original Text It Says"* is his first book. He lives with his wife Kaitlin in Oakville, Ontario, Canada.

"IN THE ORIGINAL TEXT IT SAYS"

WORD-STUDY FALLACIES AND HOW TO AVOID THEM

Benjamin J. Baxter

Energion Publications

Gonzalez, Florida

2012

Cover: Jason Neufeld (jasonneufelddesign.com)

ISBN10: 1-893729-17-6

ISBN13: 978-1-893729-17-9

Library of Congress Control Number: 2011944724

DEDICATION

To those who regularly attended my class
at Oakridge Bible Chapel:
Judy, Kaitlin, Phil and Brenda, Kim and Wendy,
Alice, Bruce and Gail, Jon and Alyssa

Table of Contents

INTRODUCTION

How often we hear (or preach) in sermons and read in books, "In the original text it says ...." Such comments usually refer to Hebrew or Greek words, the building blocks of the inspired text. How do we know if these statements are true? In practice, we tend to accept a statement about biblical word-meaning that jives with our pre-understanding of the passage, or statements made by pastors and scholars whom we respect. Yet we need to acknowledge that such a method will not necessarily yield accurate results. What we need is an ability to intelligently evaluate what we are told about the meanings of biblical words. The purpose of this book is to enable you to do exactly that.

The following pages are written primarily for the pastor who is familiar with commentaries, who has at some point in time taken at least one introductory course in both Greek and Hebrew, and who is still able to sound out words in each language. However, an attempt has been made to write this book in such a way that no knowledge of either biblical language is required in order to understand and make use of what is contained here. What this book will not give you is the knowledge required to determine the meanings of biblical words; to do so you will need to actually study the languages themselves. Instead, this book will enable you to more accurately determine which statements about words you should accept, and which ones you should reject.

In order to bring you to that point, the first part of this book explains some basic concepts about word-meaning in

every language, and then includes a list of word-study fallacies, which are mistakes that are made when those basic
concepts are ignored. The second part of this book then shows
you how to apply the knowledge gained in the first part by
walking you through statements about Hebrew and Greek
word-meaning in commentaries aimed at pastors.

PART A: OH THE WORDS WE MEET[1]

Within this first part of the book is an explanation of five basic concepts related to word-meaning in any language, and a list of six word-study fallacies. English, Hebrew, and Greek examples of the concepts and fallacies are given throughout to aid in comprehension and to show that the fallacies are indeed problematic in each language.

A Few Words on Words

Words have a range of meaning.

Each individual word is usually used in different ways with various meanings, and therefore has a range of meaning. Consider the range of meaning of the word *bank*: a person will deposit money in a *bank*, or give blood to a blood *bank*. You could install a *bank* of lights, fall over a *bank* (either of snow or dirt), or walk through a *bank* of fog. Used as a verb, an airplane can *bank* to the right, a person can *bank* money, and it is possible to *bank* a basketball off a backboard. When a statement is trustworthy a person might even be told, "You can *bank* on it."

The same word-form, *bank*, can be used as both a noun and a verb with a variety of meanings. Some of the uses of

---

[1]   In this first section I draw heavily from Baxter 2009-10 and 2010-11. The reader who has at least a first-year level understanding of Hebrew or Greek is encouraged to read these articles for a more advanced discussion of the issues presented in this section, as well as an explanation of how to determine the meanings of Hebrew and Greek words.

bank above can be seen to be related, but some are unrelated to each other. For instance, there is an obvious connection between *bank* in "deposit money in a *bank*" and "give blood to a blood *bank*." Both uses of *bank* refer to the place where something is collected or stored, whether that something be money or blood. Yet, these two uses of *bank* are apparently unrelated to *bank* in "a *bank* of lights," which refers to a series of objects lined up in a row, and *bank* in "an airplane can *bank* to the right." Notice also that these additional uses of *bank* are unrelated to each other.

As a further example of the various uses of words, consider the word *ball* in the following two sentences...

- Kick the *ball* into the net.

- I had a wonderful time dancing at the *ball*.

In these two sentences, the same word *ball* is used with two completely different, unrelated, meanings. On the other hand, notice how *mole* is used in these two sentences...

- A *mole* likes to burrow in the ground.

- The *mole* will deliver us the information tonight.

Unlike the examples with *ball* above, these two uses of *mole*, though different in meaning, are still related because both the animal and human moles are digging for things.

HEBREW—The word כִּסֵא (*kisē'*) is used with related, though different, meanings in 2 Kings 4:10, where the Shunammite woman says of Elijah to her husband, "Let us make a small room on the roof with walls and put there for him a bed, a table, **a chair** [וְכִסֵא, *věkisē'*], and a lamp, so that whenever he comes to us, he can go in there," and in Genesis 41:40, where Pharaoh says to Joseph, "You shall be over my house, and all my people shall order themselves as you command.

Only as regards **the throne** [הַכִּסֵא, *hakisē'*] will I be greater than you."[2]

GREEK—Different, and apparently unrelated, uses of the word ξενίζω (*xenizō*) can be found in Acts 10:6, "He is **lodging** [ξενίζεται, *xenizetai*] with one Simon, a tanner, whose house is by the sea," and in 1 Peter 4:4, "With respect to this **they are surprised** [ξενίζονται, *xenizontai*] when you do not join them in the same flood of debauchery, and they malign you."

It is often difficult to determine whether different meanings of a word are related or not. Nevertheless, the important thing to note is that because words have a range of meaning, every time a word (in any language!) is found it will not necessarily carry the same meaning, nor will the meaning of a word in one context necessarily be related to the meaning of that word in another context.

Words may be used as synonyms.

A synonym is "a word or phrase that means exactly or nearly the same as another word or phrase in the same language" (*Oxford* April 2010g). Although it is unlikely that any language has absolute synonyms (i.e., words that can occur with the same meanings in all of the same contexts, but no others), there are many words whose ranges of meaning overlap, and therefore can be used as synonyms in certain contexts. Examples of English words that may be used as synonyms are *angry* and *mad* or *smile* and *grin*. The greater the overlap in the ranges of meaning of two words, the more likely they will be used synonymously. The words *sea* and *ocean* may both be used to refer to a body of salt water that surrounds the continents (e.g., the Atlantic Ocean), but of the two, only *sea* may be

---

[2]   Throughout the examples in this book, English words are bolded to indicate how each Hebrew or Greek word (or phrase) is translated.

used to refer to an expanse of salt water that is surrounded by land (e.g., the Dead Sea). In certain contexts *sea* and *ocean* may be used as synonyms, but they do not have the same range of meaning. Consider as another example the words *girl* and *wench,* which in some contexts can be used as synonyms, but often the latter word carries negative connotations of "servant" or "prostitute." Even though each word has a unique range of meaning, it is possible that in certain contexts two different words can be used interchangeably without any noticeable difference in meaning.

HEBREW—Although differing in their ranges of meaning, בָּרָא (*bārā'*) and עָשָׂה (*'āsāh*) are used without any noticeable difference of meaning in Genesis 5:1, "When God **created** [בְּרֹא, *bĕrō'*] man, **he made** [עָשָׂה, *'āsāh*] him in the likeness of God" (cf. Gen 2:4).

GREEK—The words λόγος (*logos*) and ῥῆμα (*hrēma*), though having different ranges of meaning, are used synonymously in Luke 9:44, "Let these **words** [λόγους, *logous*] sink into your ears: The Son of Man is about to be delivered into the hands of men," and in Luke 24:11, "but these **words** [ῥήματα, *hrēmata*] seemed to [the apostles] an idle tale, and they did not believe them" (with "these words" being the things told them by the women who saw Jesus' tomb empty).

When the ranges of meaning of two words overlap, they may be used as synonyms in certain contexts.

A word's meaning is controlled by its context

The reality that each word has a range of meaning leads to the question, "How is a word's meaning determined?" The answer is: context. If someone were to ask you, "What does the word *bank* mean?" you would probably respond with something like, "In what context?" or "Read me a sentence with *bank* in it." This is because, even though you might very well be fully aware of the word *bank*'s range of meaning, the meaning of *bank* will only be a part of that range of meaning in any given context.

The context necessary to determine a word's meaning includes the words with which it is connected in a sentence, and often much more. For example, in the sentence, "Frederick slid down the snow bank," it is clear that *bank* means "a long, high mass or mound of a particular substance" (*Oxford* April 2010a), because *bank* is preceded by the words "slid down the snow." It may at first seem that *snow* is sufficient to indicate that *bank* is a mass of some substance, but this is not actually the case. A snow bank could conceivably refer, at least in a fictional world, to a building in which people deposit snow for future use. Therefore, it is not just *snow bank*, but the fact that Frederick slid down this snow bank that we know a mass of snow is in view.

There are times, however, when the sentence in which a word occurs is not sufficient to determine its meaning. For example, consider this: "Genevieve walked into the bank." There are multiple possibilities for the meaning here of *bank*. The bank that Genevieve walked into could be a financial institution, a snow bank, or even the previously-mentioned bank where snow is stored for future use. A larger context than the sentence is needed in order to determine the meaning of *bank* in this instance.

As another example of how a word's meaning is controlled by the context in which it is found, consider the word *old* as it could be used to describe a church by two friends. We can imagine one of the friends pointing to the church and saying, "That is an old church." The other friend could respond with, "That is my old church." In these two statements, *old* is used with different meanings. In the first case ("an old church"), *old* refers to how long the church has existed, meaning something like *having existed for a long time*, but in the second case ("my old church"), *old* refers to a church that the person previously attended, meaning something like *from a previous time in one's life*. A person who has left a church to attend a different church could refer to the first church as "my old church" even if they only stopped attending it a month prior. A church building, however, on which construction was completed only one month prior, could not normally be referred to as "an old church." The meaning of *old* in each case is influenced by its immediate context.

If *cheese* is substituted for *church* in the above sentences, we are left with "That is an old cheese" and "That is my old cheese." In these two sentences, where it is *cheese* that is described as *old*, *old* refers in both cases to a particular type of cheese. In the second sentence, *old* does not mean *from a former time in one's life*, even though the structure of the sentence is the same as "That is my old church," where *old* did mean *from a former time in one's life*. In each of the above four uses of *old*, its meaning is impacted by the other words in the sentences. It is through the examination of the context in which a word occurs that its meaning is determined.[3]

HEBREW—The word קֹול (*qôl*) has a range of meanings that can be rendered in English through words such as *voice, noise,* and *thunder.* It occurs with the sense of *audible vibrations moving through the air* in Genesis 3:8, "And they heard the **sound** [קֹול, *qôl*] of the Lord God walking in the garden in the cool of the day," where the meaning of the word is determined by the fact that it is "the Lord God walking" that is heard. The same word occurs in Deuteronomy 5:25, which reads, "If

---

[3]   The following Hebrew and Greek examples do not show all of the necessary steps for determining the meaning of a biblical word. Rather, the purpose of the examples is simply to demonstrate how context influences the meaning of a word. For the full explanation of how to determine the meaning of a Hebrew or Greek word, see Baxter 2009-10.

we hear the …[קֹול, qôl]… of the Lord our God any more, we shall die." This sentence alone is not sufficient to determine the meaning of קֹול (qôl). The surrounding context, however, makes it clear that it is God's *voice* that is heard by the Israelites, for God's קֹול (qôl) was heard "speaking" (Deut 5:26).

ADVANCED INFORMATION—The word קֹול (qôl) is able to serve as a good example of the challenge of determining the meaning of a biblical word. Since we have limited material with which to work, it is not always possible to determine the exact meaning of a biblical word. For example, in 1 Samuel 26, David and his men sneak down to King Saul's camp while he and his army are sleeping, steal his spear and water jar, and leave. Then from the safety of a distant hill, David calls down to the commander of Saul's army, Abner, and says in part, "As the LORD lives, you deserve to die, because you have not kept watch over your lord, the LORD's anointed" (1 Sam 26:16). The next verse then says, "Saul recognized David's קֹול [qôl]." At this point it may seem like *a human being's voice* is the obvious way to understand קֹול (qôl) in 1 Samuel 26:17. However, קֹול (qôl) can also be used to refer to the sound of a trumpet, such as in Exodus 19:19, "And as the קֹול [qôl] of the trumpet grew louder and louder …." In 1 Samuel 26:17, קֹול (qôl) is limited by "David's" to refer to the sound of this particular man's voice, as distinct from the voice of any other human being. Since a trumpet has a sound that is distinct from other musical instruments, such as a tuba or a clarinet, is it possible that קֹול (qôl) means the same thing when used of both David and a trumpet, something like *the distinct quality of sound emitted from an opening*? That opening in 1 Samuel 26:17 would be David's mouth, whereas it would be the part of a trumpet where the sound comes out in Exodus 19:19. The use of קֹול (qôl) in Genesis 3:8 to refer to the sound made by God while walking in the garden would have a different meaning, since the sound of walking would not be *a distinct quality of sound emitted from an opening*. On the other hand, it is possible that קוֹל (*qôl*) is to be understood as *a human being's voice* when used in reference to the sound of both a person speaking and a trumpet, with the latter described anthropomorphically. There are many times when the exact meaning of a biblical word cannot be determined, so it is important to recognize to what degree of accuracy the meaning of a word can be stated. Even though the meaning of קוֹל (*qôl*) may be hard to determine, it is clear that it is used to refer to David's voice in 1 Samuel 26:17 and the sound of a trumpet in Exodus 19:19.

GREEK—The word παραιτέομαι (*paraiteomai*) has an interesting range of meanings. One way in which it is used can be seen in Mark 15:6, "Now at the feast [Pilate] used to release for them one prisoner for whom **they asked** [παρῃτοῦντο, *parētounto*]." The context allows us to see that something like "asked" or "requested" is the sense of the word here. In v 8 (different word) the crowd "began **to ask** [αἰτεῖσθαι, *aiteisthai*] Pilate to do as he usually did for them," in v 9 Pilate asks if they want him to release Jesus for them, and then in v 15, "Pilate, wishing to satisfy the crowd, released for them Barabbas."

Now consider how παραιτέομαι (*paraiteomai*) is used in 1 Timothy 4:7, "**Have nothing to do with** [παραιτοῦ, *paraitou*] irreverent, silly myths. Rather train yourself for godliness." What is interesting about παραιτέομαι (*paraiteomai*) is that it is used with virtually polar opposite meanings in the above two verses. If the meaning of παραιτέομαι (*paraiteomai*) in Mark 15:6 was taken as its meaning in 1 Timothy 4:7, the resulting modified ESV translation would be

"**Request** irreverent, silly myths. Now[4] train yourself for godliness." This understanding of παραιτέομαι (*paraiteomai*) can be seen to be incorrect for the reasons that requesting *irreverent* myths is inconsistent with training oneself in *godliness*, and because in 1 Timothy 1:4 Timothy is told to charge certain people not "to devote themselves to myths." The particular context in which παραιτέομαι (*paraiteomai*) is found is what controls its meaning. The meaning of a word is controlled by the context in which it is found.

Related to the issue of how context impacts word-meaning (specifically, how words are used in combination with one another for determining meaning) is the occurrence of idioms. An idiom is "a group of words established by usage as having a meaning not deducible from those of the individual words" (*Oxford* April 2010d). English examples of idioms include "to pull a fast one," "to relieve oneself," "to sleep with," "to pass away," "on the up and up," and "a chip on one's shoulder." Notice that the meanings of these idioms cannot be determined simply by adding together the meanings of each individual word; rather, the entire phrase has a single meaning.

HEBREW—Examples of Hebrew idioms can be found in 1 Samuel 24:3 (Hebrew, 24:4), "…there was a cave, and Saul went in to relieve himself [Hebrew: went in *to cover his feet*]," and in 1 Kings 14:10, "I [Yahweh] will bring harm upon the house of Jeroboam and will cut off from Jeroboam every male [Hebrew: every *one urinating on a wall*]."

GREEK—Greek idioms are found in Matthew 10:27, "… what you hear whispered [Greek: hear *in the ear*], proclaim on the housetops," and James 1:23, "…he is like a man who looks

---

[4] The Greek word here is δέ (*de*), which is appropriately translated as "now" if παραιτέομαι (*paraiteomai*) is rendered as "request" in 1 Timothy 4:7.

intently at his natural face [Greek: at *the face of his birth*] in a mirror."

Many words change meaning over time.

As any language is used, many of the words within that language change meaning. For example, a relatively recent change of meaning has occurred with the English word *gay*. At one time, *gay* was often used to mean something like "light-hearted" or "brightly coloured" (*Oxford* April 2010c), such as in the well-known Christmas carol, *Deck the Halls*: "Don we now our gay apparel." This meaning of the word *gay* has, however, fallen out of modern English usage, with the word taking on the meaning of "homosexual." The fact that words change meaning is significant for determining the meaning of a word in a particular occurrence. If a piece of writing contained the question, "Should gay marriages be promoted?", the time period from which this writing came would be essential information for determining if the question was referring to *happy* marriages or to *homosexual* marriages. Similarly, the English word *nice*, which can be used in a complimentary way in a sentence such as, "She looks nice today," is derived from the Latin word *nescius,* which has a non-complimentary meaning along the lines of "ignorant" (Silva 1983, 38). Similarly non-complimentary was the use of *nice* in Middle English with the sense of "stupid" (*Oxford* April 2010e). Since many words change meaning over time, the time-period in which a piece of literature was written is part of the context that controls word-meaning.

HEBREW and **GREEK** examples of words changing meaning over time can be found below, in fallacy #2.

Meaning is different than translation

In the sentence, "I deposited my paycheque in the bank," the word *bank* means "a financial establishment that uses money deposited by customers for investment, pays it out when required, makes loans at interest, and exchanges currency" (*Oxford* April 2010b). The French word that could be appropriately used in the above context is *banque*, but *banque* and *bank* do not mean the same thing, because they do not share the same range of meaning. It is not possible to install a *banque* of lights, nor will an airplane *banque* to the right; *banque* does not exactly parallel (i.e., it is not used in all of the same contexts with the same meaning, and no others) the meaning of *bank*. The words *banque* and *bank* serve as an example of the fact that determining how to translate a word is different than determining the meaning of a word. Although it is possible for two words in different languages to share the same range of meaning, this possibility is highly unlikely, and certainly cannot be assumed to be true.

HEBREW—Although *glory* is used to translate כָּבוֹד (*kābôd*) in Exodus 16:10, "And as soon as Aaron spoke to the whole congregation of the people of Israel, they looked toward the wilderness, and behold, the **glory** [כְּבוֹד, *kĕbôd*] of the LORD appeared in the cloud," the two words do not mean the same thing, as can be seen by the fact that *glory* would be an inappropriate English word to use to translate כָּבוֹד (*kābôd*) in Genesis 31:1, "Now Jacob heard that the sons of Laban were saying, 'Jacob has taken all that was our father's, and from what was our father's he has gained all this **wealth** [הַכָּבֹד, *hakābōd*]'," (with *wealth* referring to the many material possessions Jacob has acquired).

GREEK—Those seeking support for the doctrine of the rapture may wish to argue that the word *rapture* occurs in 1 Thessalonians 4:17, "Then we who are alive, who are left, **will be caught up** [ἁρπαγησόμεθα, *harpagēsometha*—a form of ἁρπάζω, *harpazō*] together with them in the clouds to meet the Lord in the air, and so we will always be with the Lord."

However, *rapture* does not mean the same thing as ἁρπάζω (*harpazō*), as can be seen from the use of ἁρπάζω (*harpazō*) in John 6:15, "Perceiving then that they were about to come and **take** him **by force** [ἁρπάζειν, *harpazein*] to make him king, Jesus withdrew again to the mountain by himself" (cf. Acts 8:39-40, where Peter is "raptured" by the Spirit of the Lord, only to find himself in Azotus. Has the rapture already happened? Or should we anticipate that when we are raptured we may end up in Azotus, or some other town, rather than with Jesus?).

No English word, including *God, Jesus,* and *apostle*, occurs in the manuscripts of the Bible, since biblical manuscripts were written in Hebrew, Aramaic, and Greek. English words are different than Hebrew and Greek words, and so should not be equated. It should come as no surprise, then, that the primary goal of studying biblical words is to determine their meanings in the contexts in which they occur so as to better understand each passage of Scripture, whether the meaning of the passage can be adequately conveyed in English or not.

Word-Study Fallacies

All Meanings Lead to Rome

The first fallacy is committed when it is assumed that every single use of a particular word can be traced back to, and its meaning derived from, one basic meaning. Some find this basic meaning in a word's root, which could naturally lead to the suggestion that since *awe* is the root of *awful*, then someone who calls food *awful* is filled with wonder and amazement by how it tastes. Yet if I were to eat Brussels sprouts-flavoured ice cream I would be inclined to call it *awful* without being surprised or amazed by the ice cream's taste.

Words that share the same root may be related in meaning, but a word's root is not a definite indicator of its meaning.

HEBREW—It would be incorrect to suggest that because לֶחֶם (leḥem, bread) and מִלְחָמָה (milḥāmāh, war) share the same root (לחם, lḥm), *every* war is essentially a struggle for food (Barr 2004, 102).

GREEK—Since κοπιάω (kopiaō, to work) and κόπος (kopos, trouble) share the same root (κοπ-, kop-), does this demonstrate that working only causes trouble and hardship in one's life?

A second way in which the *All Meanings Lead to Rome* fallacy can occur is when the supposed basic meaning of an English word is applied to the meaning of the word(s) that it translates. Barr gives the example of the word *holy*, which some claim means "healthy, sound, whole." This supposed basic meaning is then read into every context in which the word *holy* is used to translate a Hebrew or Greek word (e.g. קָדוֹשׁ, qādôš, or ἅγιος, hagios). Therefore, the injunction from God, "be holy, for I am holy," (Lev 11:44-45; cf. 1 Pet 1:16) is taken as a command to be whole or healthy, rather than to be like God.[5] As Barr points out, this interpretation of what it means to be holy is based entirely upon English rather than a study of Hebrew or Greek (Barr 2004, 112; cf. 166). It is incorrect to assume that the meaning of a Hebrew or Greek word is the same as a supposed basic meaning of an English word.

---

[5]   "The term *holy* is often linked to the semantic range of *separateness*, that is, it communicates that God is totally other, just as holy things are 'set apart' for God's use. Fundamentally, however, the term *holy* refers to what is divine and not created, and what is holy is defined as 'that which belongs to the sphere of God's being or activity' " (Boda 2009, 51, who is quoting from Jenson 1992, 48).

Time Warp

The second fallacy occurs when the meaning of a word is "warped" by deriving it either from an earlier time period or from a later time period than the occurrence in question. When the meaning of a word is derived from an earlier time period it is often said to be what the word "really means." This particularly occurs with compound words, i.e., words that are composed of two (or more) words joined together. It is often suggested that the meanings of these words are determined by simply adding the meanings of the two words together, since "that is where the word originally came from." The difference in meaning between "overhang" and "hangover" should show the error in such thinking; which word is appropriate for an awning that both *over* your head *hangs*, and *hangs over* your head?; and which word is appropriate for the effects of drinking that *hang over* to the next day, and which *over* your head *hang* like a dark storm cloud? Similarly, should we believe that a "butterfly" is churned cream that has grown wings?

HEBREW—Barr gives the Hebrew example of those who interpret the divine name שַׁדַּי (*šaday*, almighty) as meaning "the sufficient one" due to its supposed derivation from the relative pronoun שַׁ (*ša*, who) and the word דַּי (*day*, enough) (Barr 2004, 110n2).

GREEK—The word ἀναγινώσκω (*anaginōskō*, to read) does not mean "to know more than," despite the common glosses[6] given for its component parts ("upwards, up" for ἀνά, *ana*, with verbs, and "to know" for γινώσκω, *ginōskō*).

The meaning of a compound word *may* be determined by combining the meanings of its component parts, but this must be discovered from the uses of the word, rather than simply be assumed to be true.

---

[6]   A gloss is an English word-substitute.

It is possible not only for *Time Warp* to occur by looking back in time, but also by looking forward in time. This happens when a word's meaning is derived from a later time period. In order to understand the problem with this method from an English perspective, consider the word *nephew*. Even though I can now use the word *nephew* to refer to my brother's (or sister's) son, once upon a time it was used to refer to the son of someone's son (or daughter), i.e., a grandson (*Merriam* 2010; Carson 1996, 35n21). This information allows us to see that I would be grossly misinterpreting the author of a piece of literature from this "once upon a time" if I concluded that a child who was called the nephew of his grandfather was thereby a product of an incestuous relationship between this grandfather's brother and this grandfather's daughter (thereby being both the uncle and the grandfather of the child). Words change meaning over time, so a later meaning of a word cannot be assumed to be the meaning of that word in an earlier time period.

HEBREW—The fact that the word חַשְׁמַל (*ḥašmal*) can be used similar to the English *electricity* in Modern Hebrew is entirely irrelevant for determining its meaning in Ezekiel 1:4, "As I looked, behold, a stormy wind came out of the north, and a great cloud, with brightness around it, and fire flashing forth continually, and in the midst of the fire, as it were gleaming **metal** [הַחַשְׁמַל, *haḥašmal*]."[7] Since electricity was not available for use in Ezekiel's day, this meaning of חַשְׁמַל (*ḥašmal*) cannot be imposed upon the use of the word in Ezekiel 1:4.

GREEK—The fact that *dynamite* is derived from the Greek word δύναμις (*dynamis*) is sometimes thought to aid understanding of Romans 1:16, "For I am not ashamed of the gospel, for it is the **power** [δύναμις, *dynamis*] of God for

---

[7]Thanks to Dr. Mark Boda for this example.

salvation to everyone who believes, to the Jew first and also to the Greek." However, dynamite was not invented until the 1800s AD by Alfred Nobel, so there is no way that Paul would have had the destructive power of dynamite in mind when speaking of the life-giving power of the gospel (*Encyclopædia* 2009).

Swamp Water[8]

The third fallacy is committed by taking a word in a particular context to say far more than it actually does, filling it with multiple meanings or information that is actually found apart from the word itself. One way this fallacy can be seen is when information that limits or clarifies the meaning of a word in a given context is taken to be part of the word's meaning. For instance, in the sentence, "Jesus saved Peter from his sins," the word *saved* itself does not mean *to deliver someone from the punishment for sin*. A person can be saved from many different dangers, whether that danger be drowning, burning in a fire, or punishment (either for wrongdoing or for being wrongfully accused). It is the context of the sentence, passage, or entire discourse that will indicate from what a person is being saved.

HEBREW—In Ezekiel 11:2 the prophet is told, "Son of man, these are the men who devise iniquity and who give wicked **counsel** [עֲצַת, *'ăṣat*] in this city." From this verse, it could be suggested that the word עֵצָה (*'ēṣāh*) refers to counsel that is given in a city, since the counsel in Ezekiel 11:2 was given in a city. This erroneous conclusion could lead to the idea that Psalm 1:1 teaches us that if we want to avoid wicked counsel, then we should not spend any time in cities, because the verse uses the same word for counsel as does Ezekiel 11:2:

---

8   The name of this fallacy is from Boda 2004, 2; it refers to the practice of mixing multiple types of pop or juice to make a beverage that looks like water from a swamp.

"Blessed is the man who walks not **in the counsel** [בַּעֲצַת, ba'ăṣat] of the wicked, nor stands in the way of sinners, nor sits in the seat of scoffers."

GREEK—It could be suggested that ὁ λαός (*ho laos*) always refers to the Israelites because Hebrews 11:25 says that Moses chose "rather to be mistreated **with the people** [τῷ λαῷ, *tō laō*] of God than to enjoy the fleeting pleasures of sin." This misunderstanding of the word λαός (*laos*) could then lead to the conclusion that Titus 2:14 teaches that only Israelites can be redeemed by the blood of Jesus: "[Jesus] gave himself for us to redeem us from all lawlessness and to purify for himself **a people** [λαὸν, *laon*] for his own possession who are zealous for good works."

Each word contributes meaning to the sentence in which it is found, but that word's meaning does not include the meanings of the other words in the sentence.

A second place that *Swamp Water* can be found is when information gleaned from a number of different contexts in which the same word is used is collectively said to be the meaning of the word. For example, it could be claimed that the word *robber* always refers to a white man wearing a mask who has a gun and steals diamonds, due to the following sentences:

- ✔ The robber reached his white hand into the broken display case and snatched up a diamond necklace.

- ✔ The gun in the robber's hand pointed menacingly in the grill of the employee.

- ✔ As he stepped into view of the camera, the robber's mask covered all but his cold eyes.

It might then be suggested that the sentence "The robber cut her arm during the escape" implies that this woman views herself as a man. It may be true that the woman in question views herself in some way as a man, but this has nothing to do with the fact that she is called a *robber.*

HEBREW—One might be tempted to suggest that אֶרֶץ (*'ereṣ,* land) means *a wasteland filled with wild beasts,* because of the following passages: "Behold the **land** [אֶרֶץ, *'ereṣ*] of the Chaldeans! This is the people that was not; Assyria destined it for wild beasts. They erected their siege towers, they stripped her palaces bare, they made her a ruin" (Isa 23:13; cf. Ezek 14:15), and Jeremiah 2:15: "The lions have roared against him; they have roared loudly. They have made **his land** [אַרְצוֹ, *'arṣô*] a waste; his cities are in ruins, without inhabitant" (cf. Jer 4:7). The fact that a particular אֶרֶץ (*'ereṣ,* land) is a wasteland or that it is filled with wild beasts may be true, but this will be irrespective of the word אֶרֶץ (*'ereṣ,* land) itself.

GREEK—Carson reminds us that some take ἀγαπάω (*agapaō,* to love) to mean: "an act of willed self-sacrifice for the good of another" (Carson 2000, 26), like the kind of love that God has, due to passages such as Ephesians 5:2, "And walk in love, as Christ **loved** [ἠγάπησεν, *ēgapēsen*] us and gave himself up for us, a fragrant offering and sacrifice to God," and Luke 6:35, "But **love** [ἀγαπᾶτε, *agapate*] your enemies, and do good, and lend, expecting nothing in return, and your reward will be great, and you will be sons of the Most High, for he is kind to the ungrateful and the evil." However, such an understanding of the word ἀγαπάω (*agapaō,* to love) makes it difficult to understand why (in Luke 11:43) Jesus would pronounce "Woe!" against the Pharisees because they "**love** [ἀγαπᾶτε, *agapate*] the best seat in the synagogues and greetings in the marketplaces." Why would Jesus condemn the type of love that God has, especially if the Pharisees' seating choice was a sacrificial act? It is also hard to understand how "an act of willed self-sacrifice for the good of another" is help-ful for understanding the verb in 2 Peter 2:15, "They have followed the way of Balaam, the son of Beor, who **loved** [ἠγάπησεν, ēgapēsen] gain from wrongdoing" (cf. LXX 2 Sam 13:4, 14-15, where Amnon rapes Tamar, whom he "loves").

Individual words do not mean the same thing as the in-formation found in multiple sentences where that word is used.

A third way that *Swamp Water* is evident is when different meanings (or English glosses) of a word are gathered and all are taken to be relevant for understanding the meaning of that word in a particular context. For instance, consider the sen-tence: "the man walked out of the house and placed his dirty socks in the basin." A *basin* can be a wide shallow vessel used for holding liquids, or an area of land drained by rivers (e.g., the Amazon Basin). It would be incorrect to argue that since the man placed his socks in a *basin*, this meant that the water presumed to be in that basin would be poured out into a nearby river, simply because the word *basin* was used in the sentence.

HEBREW—One might (incorrectly) suggest that the unre-deemed בַּיִת (*bayit*) in Leviticus 25:30, which remains in the possession of its buyer after the Year of Jubilee, refers both to the *dwelling place* and the *family* who lives in it because both of those meanings are given in a lexicon for בַּיִת (*bayit*).

GREEK—In the Parable of the Weeds in Matthew 13:24-30, an enemy plants weeds in a man's wheat field. When the wheat grows up, Matthew 13:26 tells us that weeds also ἐφάνη (*ephanē*—a form of φαίνω, *phainō*), but it would then be wrong to suggest that the servants could tell the weeds had ap-peared because they were shining, simply because "to appear" and "to shine" are glosses commonly found in a lexicon for φαίνω (*phainō*).

Lost in Translation

The fourth fallacy lies in assuming that a word's range of meaning in one language will be perfectly matched by the range of a word's meaning in another language. A common example of getting *Lost in Translation* is when the meaning of a Greek word in the Septuagint (LXX—the Koine Greek translation of the OT) is assumed to be equivalent to the meaning of the Hebrew word that it translates.[9] An examination of the LXX is often helpful in biblical study, but it cannot simply be assumed that a Greek word in the LXX and the Hebrew word that it translates are equivalent in meaning. This fallacy can be made from two different perspectives: a person studying a word in the Hebrew Bible may check the LXX to see how it has been translated; similarly, someone studying a word in the Greek New Testament may find that word in the LXX and then check to see what Hebrew word it translates. From either perspective, caution is essential when studying the LXX to determine the meaning of either a Hebrew or a Greek word, for at least the following reasons:

✔ The books of the LXX evidence differing translation styles (e.g., following the order of the Hebrew words vs. following a more natural Greek style).

✔ There is no way of knowing for certain what Hebrew text was used in the translation of any book of the LXX. For example, Genesis 2:2 reads, "And on **the seventh [הַשְּׁבִיעִי**, *haševî'î*] day God finished his work that he had done, and he rested on the seventh day from all his work that he had done." The LXX, on the other hand, says that God finished his work on **the sixth [τῇ ἕκτῃ**, *tȩ̄ hektȩ̄*] day. It is difficult to know

---

[9]   For an introduction to the relationship between the MT (Masoretic Text) and the LXX for determining word-meaning, see: Silva 1983, 53-73; Groom 2003, 73-91.

whether the LXX translator was using a Hebrew text which differed from the Masoretic Text (MT), or whether the change in day on which God completed his work was made in the LXX out of a desire to clarify that God did not work on the seventh day.

It must be stressed that even if it can be safely assumed that it is known which Hebrew text lies behind a particular LXX translation, the Greek word and the Hebrew word it translates cannot be equated in meaning. For example, Romans 3:23-25 says,

> for all have sinned and fall short of the glory of God, and are justified by his grace as a gift, through the redemption that is in Christ Jesus, whom God put forward as **a propitiation** [ἱλαστήριον, *hilastērion*] by his blood, to be received by faith. This was to show God's righteousness, because in his divine forbearance he had passed over former sins.

There is great debate among scholars over the meaning of the word ἱλαστήριον (*hilastērion*) in this passage. The only other occurrence of it in the NT is in Hebrews 9:3-5, where we read,

> Behind the second curtain was a second section called the Most Holy Place, having the golden altar of incense and the ark of the covenant covered on all sides with gold, in which was a golden urn holding the manna, and Aaron's staff that budded, and the tablets of the covenant. Above it were the cherubim of glory overshadowing **the mercy seat** [τὸ ἱλαστήριον, *to hilastērion*]. Of these things we cannot now speak in detail.

In the LXX, ἱλαστήριον (*hilastērion*) is the only word
used to refer to the mercy seat, which in Hebrew is כַּפֹּרֶת
(*kapōret*). It would be wrong, however, to conclude from this
that ἱλαστήριον (*hilastērion*) means the same thing as כַּפֹּרֶת
(*kapōret*), and thus in Romans 3:25 ἱλαστήριον (*hilastērion*)
should be translated *mercy seat*. There are a couple of reasons
why this conclusion would be erroneous:

- ✔ ἱλαστήριον (*hilastērion*) is also used in the LXX to
  refer to the rims or ledges around the altar in Ezekiel
  43:14, 17 (עֲזָרָה, *ʾăzārāh*), and to the capitals (כַּפְתּוֹר,
  kaptôr) of the pillars in Amos 9:1. At the very least, this
  suggests that the semantic range of ἱλαστήριον
  (*hilastērion*) may be broader than *mercy seat* (i.e., assuming that ἱλαστήριον [*hilastērion*] is an appropriate
  word to use in Ezekiel 43:14, 17; and Amos 9:1).

- ✔ ἱλαστήριον (*hilastērion*) is used in Koine Greek literature to refer to things other than the mercy seat on the
  Ark of the Covenant (e.g., Herod's propitiatory
  [ἱλαστήριον, *hilastērion*] monument he built after being frightened in a sepulchre; Josephus, *Antiquities*,
  16.182; and the death of devout martyrs as an atoning
  sacrifice [τοῦ ἱλαστηρίου, *tou hilastēriou*] in 4 Macc
  17:22). This fact shows that in Koine Greek
  ἱλαστήριον (*hilastērion*) had a range of meaning that
  Paul was free to make complete use of in his writings.
  Therefore, it cannot be assumed that Paul uses
  ἱλαστήριον (*hilastērion*) to mean *mercy seat* in Romans 3:25 simply because it is used to translate כַּפֹּרֶת
  (*kapōret*, mercy seat) in the LXX.

It may be that in Romans 3:25, Jesus is pictured as a new
mercy seat on which blood was sprinkled for the atonement of
sins. Such an argument, however, must be based upon

contextual factors other than a simple claim that ἱλαστήριον (*hilastērion*) means the same thing as כַּפֹּרֶת (*kapōret*, mercy seat). Words in different languages are highly unlikely to have the same range of meaning—even when those languages are Hebrew and Greek.

A second way that people get *Lost in Translation* is when they assume that one English word can be used to appropriately translate any one Hebrew or Greek word in every context in which that word occurs.

HEBREW—The Hebrew word כָּנָף (*kānāp*) can often appropriately be translated into English as *wing*, such as in Isaiah 6:2, "Above [Adonai] stood the seraphim. Each had six **wings** [כְּנָפַיִם, *kĕnāpayim*]: … and with two he flew." However, to insist that כָּנָף (*kānāp*) has the same range of meaning as *wing* would lead to a bizarre understanding of Isaiah 11:12, "[Adonai] will … gather the dispersed of Judah from the four כַּנְפוֹת [*kanpôt*, **wings?**] of the earth." Are we to believe that people in Isaiah's day saw the earth as being suspended in space by four wings rather than having four corners?

GREEK—Hebrews 9:15-17 says:

> Therefore [Christ] is the mediator of a new **covenant** [διαθήκης, *diathēkēs*], so that those who are called may receive the promised eternal inheritance, since a death has occurred that redeems them from the transgressions committed under the first **covenant** [διαθήκη, *diathēkē*]. For where **a will** [διαθήκη, *diathēkē*] is involved, the death of the one who made it must be established. For **a will** [διαθήκη, *diathēkē*] takes effect only at death, since it is not in force as long as the one who made it is alive.

The author of Hebrews plays off the different meanings of διαθήκη (*diathēkē*) in order to make his argument in chapter 9. This is a play on words that cannot be captured solely with either *covenant* or *will* in English, which is why the ESV has used both in the above quotation.[10]

To force one English word to be used in every instance of a Hebrew or Greek word is to demand that the languages be more similar than they are.

A Sea of Synonyms

The fifth fallacy is a failure to recognize that words can overlap in meaning without being fully synonymous (i.e., have the same range of meaning). One way that people can flounder in *A Sea of Synonyms* is by assuming that two (or more) Hebrew or Greek words that are translated by the same English word have the same range of meaning. To understand why this is a fallacy, let us reverse the situation: the English words *Sabbath* and *week* can both be translated into Greek by the word σάββατον (*sabbaton*), but this certainly does not mean that *Sabbath* and *week* mean the same thing.

HEBREW—One could be misled into thinking that the words יָד (*yād*) and שָׂפָה (*śāpāh*) mean the same thing, because they can both be translated by the English word *bank*. See, for example, Daniel 10:4, "On the twenty-fourth day of the first month, as I was standing on the **bank** [יָד, *yad*] of the

---

10   At one time the word *testament* would have been a suitable gloss for every occurrence of διαθήκη (*diathēkē*) in Hebrews 9:15-17 (cf. KJV), but this is no longer the case. Most people are unaware that *Old Testament* at one time conveyed the meaning *Old Covenant*, and even those who are aware of this fact are not likely to say, "God made a testament with Israel." Similarly, in modern English people are only likely to use the word *testament* in the sense of a *will* in the fixed idiom *Last Will and Testament*, and some of those who use this fixed idiom are completely unaware of what *testament* means.

great river (that is, the Tigris)," and Daniel 12:5, "Then I, Daniel, looked, and behold, two others stood, one **on this bank** [לִשְׂפַת, *liśpat*] of the stream and one **on that bank** [לִשְׂפַת, *liśpat*] of the stream." Even though יָד (*yād*) and שָׂפָה (*śāpāh*) can both be translated by the word *bank* in certain contexts, these Hebrew words do not have the same range of meaning. In certain contexts, יָד (*yād*) can be translated *hand* (e.g. Dan 8:25), but שָׂפָה (*śāpāh*) cannot. In other contexts, שָׂפָה (*śāpāh*) can be translated *lip* (e.g. Dan 10:16) but יָד (*yād*) cannot.

GREEK—The words πνεῦμα (*pneuma*) and πνοή (*pnoē*) could be said to mean the same thing because they can both be translated by the word *breath* in passages like 2 Thessalonians 2:8, "And then the lawless one will be revealed, whom the Lord Jesus will kill **with the breath** [τῷ πνεύματι, *tō pneumati*] of his mouth and bring to nothing by the appearance of his coming," and Acts 17:25, "nor is he served by human hands, as though he needed anything, since he himself gives to all humankind life and **breath** [πνοήν, *pnoēn*] and everything."[11] Even though πνεῦμα (*pneuma*) and πνοή (*pnoē*) can sometimes both be translated by the word *breath*, they do not have the same range of meaning. The word πνεῦμα (*pneuma*) can be translated by the word *spirit* in reference to supernatural beings like unclean spirits (e.g. Luke 4:36), but πνοή (*pnoē*) cannot.

Multiple Hebrew or Greek words that can be translated in certain contexts by the same English word (or which have no discernible difference in meaning in certain contexts) do not thereby have the same range of meaning.

A second example of *A Sea of Synonyms* is when two Hebrew words used in a parallelism in the same grammatical

---

[11] ESV, modified.

location are assumed to mean the same thing in that context. It
is common in Hebrew to have two lines of poetry that are similar in form. An English example of a parallelism in poetry is:

> The **dogs** surround me while snarling,
>
> Growling comes as the **canines** encircle me.

The above parallelism has the form ABB'A'. In this passage, the words *dogs* and *canines* are both the subjects of the
verbs, and are used synonymously in the context. A similar
Hebrew example is found in Psalm 22:8 (Hebrew, 22:9):

> He trusts in the Lord;
> let him **deliver** him [יְפַלְּטֵהוּ, *yĕpalĕṭēhû*];
>
> let him **rescue** him [יַצִּילֵהוּ, *yaṣîlēhû*],
> for he delights in him!

Here again we have the same ABB'A' structure, where the
Hebrew verbs פִּלֵּט (*pilēṭ*—the verb in the first line) and הִצִּיל
(*hiṣîl*—the verb in the second line) are used synonymously.
The verb-change between the two lines of poetry is for stylist-
ic reasons; there is no noticeable difference in meaning in this
context between the two verbs (similar to the case with *dogs*
and *canines* above). Although words that share the same grammatical location in a parallelism are often used synonymously,
it cannot be assumed that this is always the case. For example,
consider the following English parallelisms:

> I **leaped** for joy;
>
> I **shouted** in ecstasy.

And again:

> Your smile radiates a room like a **flower** in bloom;
>
> Like a **rose** at first light, so is your smile when I
> awake.

In the first example, the second line builds on the first, to create a picture of happiness and joy. *Leaped* and *shouted* mean entirely different things, even though they share the same grammatical location in the parallel lines. In the second example, another ABB'A' structure, *flower* is a more general word, while *rose* is more specific, naming a particular type of flower. In neither case do the words that share the same grammatical location in each parallelism mean the same thing. Consider the Hebrew parallelism in Psalm 22:10 (Hebrew, 22:11):[12]

> On you was I cast **from the womb** [מֵרָחֶם, *mērāḥem*],
>
> and **from the womb** [מִבֶּטֶן, *mibeṭen*] of my mother you have been my God.

The given English translation makes it appear that רֶחֶם (*reḥem*) and בֶּטֶן (*beṭen*) are used synonymously in Psalm 22:10. Throughout the Old Testament, רֶחֶם (*reḥem*) is consistently used for the place where an offspring develops in its mother, both of humans and animals, so is appropriately translated as *womb* in Psalm 22:10. However, בֶּטֶן, (*beṭen*) is used not only in contexts similar to those of רֶחֶם (*reḥem*), but also for the abdominal area of men and one animal (with no specific reference to the womb—Job 40:16). For example, Judges 3:21 reads "And Ehud reached with his left hand, took the sword from his right thigh, and thrust it **into his** [Eglon's] **belly** [בְּבִטְנוֹ, *bĕbiṭnô*]" (cf. Pss 31:9; 44:25 [Hebrew, 31:10; 44:26]; 132:11). It seems that בֶּטֶן (*beṭen*) can be used for the abdominal region (including the genitals) of men, women, and animals, while רֶחֶם (*reḥem*) is used more specifically for a female's womb. Thus, in Psalm 22:10, there is a move from the

---

[12]   ESV has been modified to more clearly demonstrate the Hebrew parallelism. ESV has: "On you was I cast from my birth, and from my mother's womb you have been my God."

specific in the first line, to the more general in the second line, which might be conveyed in English as follows:

> *On you I was cast from the **womb**,*
>
> *And from the **belly** of my mother you have been my God.*

Two words found in a Hebrew parallelism in the same grammatical location may be used synonymously, or there may be a difference in meaning. Only by examining the parallelism itself can the relationship between the words be determined, rather than by simply assuming a synonymous relationship.

Contextual Amnesia

The sixth fallacy is the failure to recognize that every user of a language is free to make use of the entire range of a word's meaning in different contexts. *Contextual Amnesia* most often occurs when it is assumed that an author will use each word with the same meaning every single time. In terms of the Scriptures, it is thus assumed that when the meaning of a word is determined in one context (often the first occurrence of the word), it can then safely be taken as the meaning of that word in every other passage in the same book. As an English example, imagine that the following sentences commence a book:

> *Filled with **rapture** and great delight, I fell to my knees, arms raised in adoration of the one whose Word I held in my right hand. As if in a trance, I knelt in that position as I imagined the coming **rapture** when I would forever be with my Saviour.*

The first time it occurs, *rapture* means "a feeling of intense pleasure or joy" (*Oxford* April 2010f). It would be a distortion of the text, however, to suggest that based upon this fact, *rapture* also means "a feeling of intense pleasure or joy" in its second occurrence, rather than "the transporting of believers to heaven at the Second Coming of Christ" (*Oxford* April 2010f). It is common for people to use the same word with different meanings in a single piece of writing, and sometimes even within the same sentence.[13]

HEBREW—The word יוֹם (*yôm,* day) is used with two different meanings in Esther 4:16: "Go, gather all the Jews to be found in Susa, and hold a fast on my behalf, and do not eat or drink for three **days** [יָמִים, *yāmîm*], night **or day** [וָיוֹם, *vāyôm*]." In the first occurrence of יוֹם (*yôm*), it refers to a 24-hour period of time, whereas in the second reference it refers to the daylight hours of a 24-hour period of time.[14]

GREEK—Mark first uses the word ἀναβλέπω (*anablepō*) in Mark 6:41: "And taking the five loaves and the two fish he [Jesus] **looked up** [ἀναβλέψας, *anablepsas*] to heaven and said a blessing and broke the loaves and gave them to the disciples to set before the people. And he divided the two fish among them all." If an author is required to use each word with the same meaning in its every occurrence, then the following translation of Mark 10:51 needs to be modified, "And Jesus said to him, 'What do you want me to do for you?' And the blind man said to him, 'Rabbi, **let me recover my sight** [ἀναβλέψω, *anablepsō*].'" In order to be consistent, the man's request to Jesus should read, "Rabbi, **let me look up**," indicating that he has some medical condition that prevents him from

---

[13]   For an English example of a word being used with different meanings in the same sentence consider the following: "You can bank on his car sliding into the snow bank on his way to the bank."

[14]   יוֹם (*yôm,* day) can also be used in the singular in Esther to refer to a 24-hour period of time as can be seen in Esther 3:4: "And when they spoke to him **day after day** [וָיוֹם יוֹם, *yôm vāyôm*] and he would not listen to them, . . ."

looking up, rather than actually being blind. Yet this suggestion for the meaning of ἀναβλέπω (*anablepō*) in Mark 10:51
is utterly absurd (he is a "blind man"!).

An author is not required to use each word the same way
every time, but is free to make complete use of a word's entire
range of meaning.

PART B: COMMENTARIES ON WORD-MEANING

Now that we have considered how words work in general, and fallacies that can be committed when those general principles are ignored, we will utilize this information in sifting through actual statements about word-meaning. Statements to be evaluated have been taken from commentaries because they are a common source of information about biblical words for pastors. The goal of this section is to show you how to make effective use of word-meaning information contained in commentaries. In order to attain this goal, we will consider how six commentaries (three OT and three NT) discuss words, and I will explain how to evaluate that information based upon what has already been discussed in Part A. The chosen commentaries come from three commentary series largely aimed at pastors: Cornerstone Biblical Commentary (CBC), The Expositor's Bible Commentary (EBC), and the NIV Application Commentary (NIVAC). Within the text of this book, the authors' names are left out in an attempt to highlight that the statements that will be considered are reflective of what you will find in many commentaries; my intention is not to single out the authors of the commentaries chosen for discussion.

Due to space limitations, only five words from both Hebrew and Greek will be discussed as they appear in each commentary. The particular words selected have been chosen in order to demonstrate how to evaluate the kinds of statements about words that you will encounter in commentaries.

1. Old Testament (2 Chronicles 1)[15]

Verses 3-5, 9-10[16]

And Solomon, and all the assembly with him, went **to the high place** [לַבָּמָה, *labāmāh*] that was at **Gibeon** [גִּבְעֹן, *gib'ōn*], for the tent of meeting of God, which Moses the servant of the LORD had made in the wilderness, was there. (But David had brought up the ark of God from Kiriath-jearim to the place that David had prepared for it, for he had pitched a tent for it in Jerusalem.) Moreover, the bronze altar that Bezalel the son of Uri, son of Hur, had made, was there before the tabernacle of the LORD. And Solomon and the assembly **sought him**[17] **out** [וַיִּדְרְשֵׁהוּ, *vayidrěšēhû*]. ... "O LORD God, let your word to David my father be now fulfilled, for you have made me king over a people as numerous as the dust of the earth. Give me now wisdom and knowledge **to go out and come in before this people** [וְאֵצְאָה לִפְנֵי הָעָם־הַזֶּה וְאָבוֹאָה, *vě'ēṣ'āh lipnê hā'ām hazeh vě'ābô'āh*], for who can **govern** [יִשְׁפֹּט, *yišpōṭ*] this people of yours, which is so great?"

---

[15]   The three OT commentaries used in this section are CBC (2010), EBC (2010), and NIVAC (2003).

[16]   Bolded words indicate which words are used in the ESV to translate the Hebrew words that are discussed below.

[17]   It is in the ESV footnote that "him" is found; the actual ESV text reads "sought it out." I have taken "him" from the ESV footnote and inserted it here in place of "it" so that you can more easily follow the comments in the commentaries that are discussed below.

לְ בָּמָה (labāmāh)

EBC (159)—"The name 'high place' (בָּמָה, bāmāh …) reflects the fact that high places were commonly associated with hills or mountains in the broader OT world."

This quotation from EBC contains a helpful historical comment that explains the English translation of בָּמָה (bāmāh), "high place." Notice that although these places of worship were "commonly associated with hills or mountains," not every בָּמָה (bāmāh) was necessarily found on an elevated area of ground (cf. Arnold and Williamson 2005, 415). For example, notice the location of the בָּמוֹת (bāmôt—plural of בָּמָה, bāmāh) mentioned in Jeremiah 7:31, "And they have built the high places [בָּמוֹת, bāmôt] of Topheth, which is in the Valley of the Son of Hinnom…." Here the places of worship are found in a valley. We must let the context of each passage indicate whether a בָּמָה (bāmāh) is located on an elevated area or not, so as not to fall into the trap of *Lost in Translation* or *A Sea of Synonyms*.

CBC (146)—"The sanctuary proper may have been atop Nebi Samwil, 1 mile south of Gibeon."

A suggestion is made here in CBC that fits within the historical context noted by EBC that "high places were commonly associated with hills or mountains in the broader OT world," but remember that CBC is giving a *suggestion* ("may have been"); it is not necessary for a בָּמָה (bāmāh) to be located "atop" anything, as we saw already in Jeremiah 7:31.

גִּבְעוֹן (gib'ōn)

EBC (159)—"Note that the name 'Gibeon' is a cognate of 'hill,' so it is likely that the high place at Gibeon was located on an elevated plateau …."

EBC points out that "Gibeon" (גִּבְעוֹן, *gibʻōn*) is a cognate
of "hill" (גִּבְעָה, *gibʻāh*). Since the meanings of Hebrew names
are often significant, the fact that גִּבְעוֹן (*gibʻōn*) is cognate with
גִּבְעָה (*gibʻāh*) suggests that the city is likely located on an elevated area of land, but it is not necessary for the בָּמָה
(*bāmāh*) to be "located on an elevated plateau" rising above
the city that is already on an elevated area of land. Carefully
think about the information you find in commentaries; here a
helpful comment about the likely significance of the name
גִּבְעוֹן (*gibʻōn*) could easily be incorrectly applied to the בָּמָה
(*bāmāh*) located in, or near, that city.

וַיִּדְרְשֵׁהוּ (*vayidrĕšēhû*—a form of דָּרַשׁ, *dāraš*)

CBC (234)—"The Chronicler emphasizes that Solomon
and the assembly gathered 'to consult' or seek (*dāraš* ...) the
Lord (1:5). Here he uses a key term that appears throughout
his account to refer to those who are in proper relationship
with the Lord. Saul was judged as one who consulted a medium rather than the Lord (1 Chr 10:13-14). In contrast to Saul,
David brought the Ark into Jerusalem so that he could seek the
Lord (1 Chr 13:3). In his charge to Solomon, David was con-
cerned that Solomon would be a person who sought the Lord
(1 Chr 22:19; 28:9) and his commandments (1 Chr 28:8)."

There is much information here in CBC that is helpful,
but care is needed when reading it to ensure that no word-
study fallacies are committed. The first piece of helpful information is that the word דָּרַשׁ (*dāraš*) is used throughout the
books of Chronicles "to refer to those who are in proper relationship with the Lord." Notice what is *not* said; CBC does
not say that דָּרַשׁ (*dāraš*) *means* "one who is in a proper relationship with the Lord," nor does it say that דָּרַשׁ (*dāraš*) is
only used in the books of Chronicles for "those who are in
proper relationship with the Lord." Instead, דָּרַשׁ (*dāraš*) is a

word often used in Chronicles when the *subject* is a person who is "in proper relationship with the Lord." This is not actually a statement about the meaning of דָּרַשׁ (*dāraš*), but a statement about the subjects of this verb in the books of Chronicles. Based upon this helpful statement, then, you should be encouraged to anticipate the likelihood (but not certainty; only context will tell you for sure) that Solomon is here in a right relationship with God.

What remains in the CBC quotation is a number of examples from the books of Chronicles that show some ways in which דָּרַשׁ (*dāraš*) is used throughout them. The first example shows that דָּרַשׁ (*dāraš*) is not *always* used of "those who are in proper relationship with the Lord," for Saul is said in 1 Chronicles 10:13-14 to have sought (לִדְרוֹשׁ, *lidrôš*) a medium rather than (וְלֹא־דָרַשׁ, *vělō'-dāraš*) the Lord. The next three verses are examples where דָּרַשׁ (*dāraš*) is used of those who are or who are encouraged to be "in proper relationship with the Lord." The final example (1 Chr 28:8) shows that not only personal beings, like Yahweh or a medium, can be the objects of דָּרַשׁ (*dāraš*), but non-personal things can also be the objects of the verb, in this case מִצְוֹת יהוה (*miṣvōt YHWH*, commandments of Yahweh). These various contexts in which דָּרַשׁ (*dāraš*) is used hint at the variety of meanings of the verb and caution against finding a person's "proper relationship with the Lord" in the use of the verb itself.

NIVAC (379)—"The verb 'to inquire of [*drš*; lit., to seek] the LORD' is an important theme in Chronicles. It denotes an act of faith, and the goal or aim of this spiritual quest is generally to seek God's direction and help at a crucial moment in one's life (or even confirmation of an earlier divine word of instruction).

"The propensity 'to inquire' of God is one measure of the faithfulness of the leaders of Israel (e.g., 1 Chr 10:14; 2 Chr 22:9). Curiously (and sadly) Selman observes that the term is not used of Solomon again, despite his exhortation in the prayer of dedication for the temple (2 Chr 7:14). Isaiah's admonition is still pertinent for the Chronicler's audience (and the church today)—'Seek [drš] the LORD while he may be found; call on him while he is near' (Isa. 55:6)."

Here is a good example of some of the things that you will find in commentaries through which one needs to tread lightly. The first thing to notice is that the verb דָּרַשׁ (dāraš—drš in above quotation) is said to literally ("lit.") mean "to seek." You will regularly find "literally" in commentaries, so you need to know that commentators are inconsistent with their use of "literally" (even within the same commentary!) and use it to indicate a number of things, including the grammatical structure of the original text, the fact that a word is a compound word (e.g. butter + fly; pine + apple), or in this case, the most commonly-used English word to translate a Hebrew word: "to seek" for דָּרַשׁ (dāraš). Such "literal" information is often interesting and can be helpful for those who know the biblical languages to track with what the author is referring to in the text, but it is rarely helpful for understanding the meaning of the word or passage. Without a knowledge of Hebrew (or Greek for the New Testament) that allows you to understand what is meant by any particular use of "literally" in a commentary, simply gloss over this information. It will only mislead you into thinking that a "literal" meaning is what the text *really* means.

The danger in thinking that "to seek" is *really* what דָּרַשׁ (dāraš) means is that this English rendering is entirely misleading for some uses of the verb. For example, Deuteronomy 11:11-12 reads, "But the land that you are going over to

possess is a land of hills and valleys, which drinks water by
the rain from heaven, a land that the LORD your God *seeks*
[דֹּרֵשׁ, *dōrēš*]. The eyes of the LORD your God are always upon
it, from the beginning of the year to the end of the year."[18] The
use of the "literal" *seeks* confuses the meaning of the passage;
the ESV's *cares for* much more accurately conveys the meaning of דָּרַשׁ (*dāraš*) in Deuteronomy 11:12. Remember that a
word's range of meaning in one language is not likely to be
exactly paralleled by a word's range of meaning in a different
language, so you should expect each Hebrew word to be translated by various English words in different contexts. Since
meaning is different than translation, do not assume that "to
seek" will give you an accurate understanding of the meaning
of דָּרַשׁ (*dāraš*).

The second issue raised in the above quotation from NI-
VAC is an issue commonly found in commentaries: a
discussion about a theme or phrase is presented as though it is
a discussion about an individual word. The first sentence begins with, "The verb," and the second sentence begins with,
"It denotes," with the remainder of the paragraph looking as
though it is a discussion of what the verb דָּרַשׁ (*dāraš*) "denotes." Having already gone through CBC's discussion of
דָּרַשׁ (*dāraš*) you know that the verb is used in more contexts
than just ones where a person is inquiring of or seeking the
Lord, so this fact should raise a red flag in your mind when
you read this first paragraph in the NIVAC quotation. Also, if
you take a close look at the quotation, you will see that "the
verb" is translated into English as "to inquire of … the LORD."
This should alert you to the fact that NIVAC is not just discussing the verb דָּרַשׁ (*dāraš*), but more specifically passages
where "the LORD" is the object of the verb דָּרַשׁ (*dāraš*).

---

[18]   Italicized words replace the original ESV words.

So why is this significant? The fact that NIVAC is discussing a phrase rather than just a verb is significant because you do not want to fall into *Swamp Water.* You are less likely to seriously consider the context of a passage if you think that the presence of a word itself contains much theological information that is actually derived from various passages in which that word is found. The information contained here in NIVAC's first quoted paragraph can be helpful to you if you recognize that a phrase is being discussed rather than the meaning of the verb דָּרַשׁ (*dāraš*).

It is furthermore important to catch the wording in the statement that the goal of inquiring of the Lord "is generally to seek God's direction and help...." This statement is true as it stands, and is helpful to you if you recognize that "generally" implies that this is not *always* the goal of the subject of דָּרַשׁ (*dāraš*) when followed by "the LORD." In a passage like 2 Chronicles 30:18-19, דָּרַשׁ (*dāraš*) means something more like "obey" (in this case, the Passover prescriptions) rather than "seek advice from":

> For a majority of the people, many of them from Ephraim, Manasseh, Issachar, and Zebulun, had not cleansed themselves, yet they ate the Passover otherwise than as prescribed. For Hezekiah had prayed for them, saying, "May the good LORD pardon everyone who sets his heart **to seek** [לִדְרוֹשׁ, *lidrôš*] God, the LORD, the God of his fathers, even though not according to the sanctuary's rules of cleanness.

Since דָּרַשׁ (*dāraš*) only "generally" is used with "the LORD" as object to speak of someone seeking advice from God, it is imperative to examine the context of 2 Chronicles

1:5 to see whether this is true of Solomon and the assembly here or not.

In the second paragraph of the quotation from NIVAC we are told that "The propensity 'to inquire' of God is one measure of the faithfulness of the leaders of Israel," so it is significant that דָּרַשׁ (*dāraš*) is not used of Solomon again in Second Chronicles. Notice first that "to inquire" is in quotation marks, directing you to this wording in the first paragraph, to indicate that NIVAC is discussing passages in which דָּרַשׁ (*dāraš*) is found. Next, in thinking through the given information about the use of דָּרַשׁ (*dāraš*) in Chronicles, it is important to keep a few things in mind. First, since words can be used synonymously, the possibility should be considered that Solomon may be found later in Second Chronicles seeking the Lord, but with a word other than דָּרַשׁ (*dāraš*). Second, since meaning is communicated with more than just individual words, the possibility should also be considered that there may be an instance where Solomon is described doing something where דָּרַשׁ (*dāraš*), or another word used synonymously, could appropriately be used of him, even though it is not. On the other hand, however, remember CBC's comment that דָּרַשׁ (*dāraš*) is "a key term that appears throughout his account to refer to those who are in proper relationship with the Lord." Therefore, it could very well be significant that דָּרַשׁ (*dāraš*) is not used of Solomon again in Chronicles. Keep NIVAC's comment in mind as you go through the rest of Chronicles and see if this really is a turning point for Solomon, or not, in seeking the Lord.

There is one final issue to surface from NIVAC's quotation. In the midst of its discussion about דָּרַשׁ (*dāraš*) there is a reference to 2 Chronicles 7:14, which would seem to suggest that דָּרַשׁ (*dāraš*) is contained within this verse. The person who reads 2 Chronicles 7:14 in English would be further encouraged to think that דָּרַשׁ (dāraš) is there: "if my people who are called by my name humble themselves, and pray and **seek** my face and turn from their wicked ways, then I will hear from heaven and will forgive their sin and heal their land."[19] The word here is not דָּרַשׁ (dāraš) but בִּקֵּשׁ (biqēš), a word whose range of meaning overlaps with that of דָּרַשׁ (dāraš). There are two important points that come out of this. First, do not assume or trust that the given biblical references in a commentary actually contain the word that they appear to contain, because they don't always. Be encouraged by this to learn the biblical languages so that you can investigate the references yourself and examine more fully the information given in commentaries about words. Second, this occurrence of בִּקֵּשׁ (biqēš) is a good example of a passage where דָּרַשׁ (dāraš) could have been used, but was not. Let this fact further encourage you to consider, as you work through Second Chronicles, whether or not it is significant that 2 Chronicles 1:5 is the last time in the book that דָּרַשׁ (dāraš) is used of Solomon. Is this a turning point in his relationship with the Lord?

וְאֵצְאָה לִפְנֵי הָעָם־הַזֶּה וְאָבוֹאָה (vě'ēṣ'āh lipnê hā'ām hazeh vě'ābô'āh)

> CBC (233)—"**to lead them properly**. Lit., 'to go out and come in before this people' (see NLT mg), a phrase that is used in military contexts to refer to breaking camp and making camp (23:7; Josh 14:11; 1 Sam 29:6; 2 Kgs 19:27) but was also a general term for the work and business of life (Deut 28:6; 2 Kgs 19:27; Ps 121:8; Isa 37:28) or conduct in general (1 Kgs 3:7). When it is used with 'before' (lipne …), it refers to military

---

[19]   Italics added.

> leadership (Num 27:17; 1 Sam 18:16). Here it ap-
> pears parallel to 'govern.'"

Here is a particularly good discussion of a Hebrew phrase that shows a good understanding of issues impacting word-meaning, but care is still needed to ensure that you draw the correct conclusions from it. First, we find another use of "literally," this time referring to a translation that is found in the margin of the New Living Translation ("NLT mg"), and also matches the ESV translation, "to go out and come in before this people." What is being indicated here by "literally" is the structure of the Hebrew, specifically that it contains two verbs and a prepositional phrase. If you do not know enough Hebrew to understand what is being indicated through a particular use of "literally," simply gloss over this information because it will be of no beneficial use to you.

The remainder of the quotation following "literally" contains a discussion of how the phrase is used throughout the Old Testament. The wording here in CBC is slightly mislead-ing because at first glance it seems that the phrase being discussed is "to go out and come in before this people" (וְאֵצְאָה לִפְנֵי הָעָם־הַזֶּה וְאָבוֹאָה, vě'ēṣ'āh [a form of יָצָא, yāṣā'] lipnê hā'ām hazeh vě'ābô'āh [a form of בּוֹא, bô']) when it is in fact only "to go out and come in" (יָצָא, yāṣā' + בּוֹא, bô') that is under discussion. There are, however, two clues in the quotation that will allow you to pick up on this even without knowledge of Hebrew. First, the second sentence begins, "When it is used with 'before' ..."; since "it" is clearly the phrase under discussion, you should be able to recognize that the phrase itself being discussed does not include "before this people." Second, if you check the references listed in the first sentence of the quotation in your English Bible you will notice that the verses include some variation of "to go out and come in" but not of "before this people." If you read commentaries with eyes wide open you will often be able to notice details such as this that will enable you to understand clearly what the commentator is trying to say. In this case, the phrase under discussion is the Hebrew equivalent of "to go out and come in" (יָצָא, *yāṣā'* + בוֹא, *bô'*).

The remainder of the CBC quotation is most helpful, with each listed verse actually containing יָצָא (*yāṣā'*) and בוֹא (*bô'*) as would be expected. The first sentence demonstrates the various types of contexts in which יָצָא (*yāṣā'*) and בוֹא (*bô'*) are found combined together, and the various meanings created by that combination. This reveals a good understanding that word-meaning is impacted by the other words it is joined together with in a sentence, and it serves to remind you that the context in which this phrase is found will impact its meaning, since it occurs in various contexts with different meanings. The second sentence in the quotation then informs you that the phrase has a particular meaning when it is used with "before"; the "*lipne*" in brackets indicates that it is the Hebrew לִפְנֵי (*lipnê*) which is being referred to, rather than any number of words that can be translated as "before." This fact means that in 2 Chronicles 1:10 the phrase in question (the two verbs + the preposition לִפְנֵי, *lipnê*) refers to something specific: military leadership. CBC has provided you here with information that cannot be gained without a knowledge of Hebrew that allows you to examine the various contexts in which יָצָא (*yāṣā'*) and בוֹא (*bô'*) are used in combination. This CBC quotation is particularly helpful in giving you an accurate understanding of what Solomon is asking of the Lord.

The final sentence of the CBC quotation states that the discussed phrase is "parallel to 'govern'." This is a true statement, but be careful with what conclusions you draw from this. Remember that Hebrew words (or a phrase and a word) found in parallel with one another do not always mean the

same thing, although they may. The meaning of "govern"
(יִשְׁפֹּט, *yišpōṭ*) must be determined rather than assumed to be
equivalent in meaning to "to lead them properly."

ADVANCED INFORMATION—The person who examines
the references given by CBC in Hebrew may prematurely reject the statement: "When it is used with 'before' (*lipne* …), it
refers to military leadership (Num 27:17; 1 Sam 18:16)," because the word-order is slightly different in each of these
references and 2 Chronicles 1:10. The only Old Testament
verses that include a combination of יָצָא (*yāṣā'*) and בּוֹא (*bô'*)
with לִפְנֵי (*lipnê*) are Numbers 27:17, 1 Samuel 18:13, 16, and
2 Chronicles 1:10. Here is the word-order of each verse:

Numbers 27:17—subject + יָצָא (*yāṣā'*) + לִפְנֵי (*lipnê*) +
object + subject + בּוֹא (*bô'*) + לִפְנֵי (*lipnê*) + object

1 Samuel 18:13 and 16—יָצָא (*yāṣā'*) + בּוֹא (*bô'*) + לִפְנֵי
(*lipnê*) + object

2 Chronicles 1:10—יָצָא (*yāṣā'*) + לִפְנֵי (*lipnê*) + object +
בּוֹא (*bô'*)

Notice that each verse listed in CBC has a slightly different word-order (with 1 Sam 18:13 and 16 being the same).
This may cause you to question the statement that יָצָא (*yāṣā'*)
+ בּוֹא (*bô'*) refers to military leadership when used with לִפְנֵי
(*lipnê*).

There are a few reasons why CBC's statement can be af-
firmed. First, aside from the above four verses where יָצָא
(*yāṣā'*) is used with לִפְנֵי (*lipnê*) and בּוֹא (*bô'*), יָצָא (*yāṣā'*) is
much more frequently used with לִפְנֵי (*lipnê*) apart from בּוֹא
(*bô'*). Of the 13 times that we find יָצָא (*yāṣā'*) + לִפְנֵי (*lipnê*)
without בּוֹא (*bô'*), it is used 10 times to refer to a military attack or military leadership (Judg 4:14; 9:39; 1 Sam 8:20;
2 Sam 5:24; Ps 68:7 [Hebrew, 68:8]; 1 Chr 14:8, 15; 2 Chr

14:10 [Hebrew, 14:9]; 20:17, 21), twice it is used of a prophet's confrontation of someone with a prophecy (2 Chr 15:2; 28:9), and once it is used of people moving away from someone else (2 Sam 24:4) where we would expect to find מִלְּפְנֵי (*milipnê*) rather than לִפְנֵי (*lipnê*) (cf. Gen 41:46; 2 Kgs 5:27). Based upon these verses, we can conclude that יָצָא (*yāṣā'*) + לִפְנֵי (*lipnê*) refers to a prophetic confrontation, a military attack, or military leadership. Of these options, it is only military leadership that is contextually viable for 2 Chronicles 1:10.

Second, as is pointed out in the above CBC quotation, יָצָא (*yāṣā'*) + בּוֹא (*bô'*) is used without לִפְנֵי (*lipnê*) "in military contexts … (23:7; Josh 14:11; 1 Sam 29:6; 2 Kgs 19:27)." Although the meaning is different when the verbs are used with לִפְנֵי (*lipnê*), this point indicates that a military context is not incompatible with the use of these two verbs together. Third, each of the four verses that contain יָצָא (*yāṣā'*), בּוֹא (*bô'*), and לִפְנֵי (*lipnê*) make good sense when taken to refer to military leadership. Fourth, although the word-order differs in these four verses (Num 27:17; 1 Sam 18:13, 16, and 2 Chr 1:10), CBC does not say that the word-order is the same. Notice the careful wording, "When it is used with 'before' (*lipne* …)". This is a true statement; in each of the listed verses, לִפְנֵי (*lipnê*) "is used with" יָצָא (*yāṣā'*) and בּוֹא (*bô'*). Based upon these four points, we can affirm with CBC that Solomon in 2 Chronicles 1:10 is asking the Lord (in part) for the knowledge required to lead the army.

יִשְׁפֹּט (*yišpōṭ*—a form of שָׁפַט, *šāpaṭ*)

NIVAC (381)—"Both Kings and Chronicles agree on the purpose of Solomon's request: able leadership 'to govern' (*špṭ*; lit., 'judge') the people of Israel (1:10; cf. 1 Kings 3:9)."

Here again we find a use of "literally," in this case to in-dicate the most commonly-used English word to translate the Hebrew verb שָׁפַט (šāpaṭ—špṭ in the above quotation). First Kings 3:9 is listed because it is the parallel verse to 2 Chron-icles 1:10, also containing שָׁפַט (šāpaṭ).

EBC (161)—"It is significant to note that the term trans-lated 'govern' ... is the verbal form of the noun 'judge.' The relationship between judgeship and kingship is stressed re-peatedly at the outset of the Israelite monarchy (see 1 Sa 8:1-22, esp. vv. 5-6, 20). The overlap between the role of judge and king may imply that the office of king in Israel could be likened to a national (supratribal) judgeship. Along these lines, Solomon's first 'wise' act is an act of judgeship (see 1 Ki 3:16-28). In order to judge wisely, Solomon must be able to discern and apply God's will."

Since NIVAC has stated that the "literal" translation of שָׁפַט (šāpaṭ) is "judge," we are not surprised by EBC's com-ment that this verb "is the verbal form of the noun 'judge.'" Yet because each word has its own unique range of meaning, the verb שָׁפַט (šāpaṭ) will not necessarily refer to the rendering of judgements (i.e. what a judge does) in its every occurrence. Furthermore, remember that because each language is differ-ent, the Hebrew noun indicated by EBC simply with the English word *judge* will not necessarily be used in the same ways as the word *judge*. So be careful not to draw conclusions about the meaning of the word שָׁפַט (šāpaṭ) from this first statement in EBC's quotation. Where EBC's comment can be helpful is to anticipate the likelihood that שָׁפַט (šāpaṭ) can be used in judicial contexts.

An additional problem with EBC's first sentence is that שָׁפַט (šāpaṭ) is not actually "the verbal form of the noun 'judge.'" Rather, the Hebrew noun "judge" is the participial form of the verb שָׁפַט (šāpaṭ). If you keep in mind what has

already been said in the previous paragraph, this error in
EBC's statement will not cause you to make any further errors.
Nevertheless, let the knowledge that such misinformation is
found in commentaries stimulate you to learn the biblical languages and so be able to steer clear of such incorrect
statements.

The remainder of EBC's comments has a positive and a
negative aspect to it. The positive side of what EBC says is the
truth that Israelite kings did have a judicial role, and the verb
שָׁפַט (šāpaṭ) can be used for the act of rendering judgement.
For example, EBC mentions Solomon rendering judgement
between two prostitutes (1 Kgs 3:16-28), an account that con-
cludes in v 28 with "And all Israel heard of the judgment that
the king **had rendered** [שָׁפַט, šāpaṭ], and they stood in awe of
the king, because they perceived that the wisdom of God was
in him to do justice." Here is a good example of the judicial
role of Israelite kings, and the fact that שָׁפַט (šāpaṭ) can at
times be appropriately translated something like *to render
judgement* or *to judge*.

The negative aspect to EBC's comments is the implication
that שָׁפַט (šāpaṭ) *really* means *to judge*, and the further implication that שָׁפַט (šāpaṭ) clearly refers to rendering judgement in
2 Chronicles 1:10. These implications could easily give you
the impression that translations such as the ESV or the NIV
(used by EBC) are misleading by translating שָׁפַט (šāpaṭ) as
"govern" in 2 Chronicles 1:10, and leave you thinking that
now you really know what שָׁפַט (šāpaṭ) means: Solomon is
expressing the challenge of rendering correct judgements,
rather than of leading the people well.

As you consider EBC's first implication, recall that each
word has a range of meaning; this fact should make you wary
of comments that imply solely a judicial sense for שָׁפַט (šāpaṭ)

in its every occurrence, especially when your English translation of 2 Chronicles 1:10 would suggest otherwise. As for the
second implication, if a commentary makes a statement that
seems to suggest that a biblical word clearly means one thing,
but that "one thing" is at odds with your English Bible, ask
yourself the question, "If this is what the word *clearly* means,
then why did the translators of my Bible not just write that?"
No translation is perfect, so you should not reject what a commentary says simply because it differs from your translation;
we learned from CBC's discussion of "to go out and come in
before this people" a meaning for the Hebrew phrase that you
would not likely draw from your English Bible. However, in
that case, CBC discussed the phrase's range of meaning and
gave a meaning for the phrase when used with a particular preposition, rather than suggesting the meaning was clear and
obvious to all. In this particular case of EBC's discussion of
שָׁפַט (*šāpaṭ*), the judicial sense of the word is all that is discussed, and it is implied that this judicial sense is the clear
meaning of the verb in 2 Chronicles 1:10, apparently because
it "is the verbal form of the noun 'judge.'" It is this implied
clear meaning of the verb that should raise a warning flag in
your mind. Remember that even though Israelite kings did
have a judicial role, and even though שָׁפַט (*šāpaṭ*) can be used
to mean *to render judgement*, these two factors do not necessarily mean that the verb means *to render judgement* in
2 Chronicles 1:10.

   There are, in fact, reasons to believe that שָׁפַט (*šāpaṭ*)
means something other, or more, than *to render judgement* in
2 Chronicles 1:10. Aside from its use in judicial contexts, שָׁפַט
(*šāpaṭ*) can also be used in broader leadership or ruling contexts. For example, the judges in the book of Judges had no
clear judicial role, but rather exercised military leadership, a
leadership that is often described with the verb שָׁפַט (*šāpaṭ*),

such as in Judges 3:10, "The Spirit of the LORD was upon [Othniel], **and he judged** [וַיִּשְׁפֹּט, *vayišpōṭ*] Israel. He went out to war, and the LORD gave Cushan-rishathaim king of Mesopotamia into his hand. And his hand prevailed over Cushan-rishathaim." We also find שָׁפַט (*šāpaṭ*) used for general leadership in Daniel 9:12a, "He has confirmed his words, which he spoke against us and against **our rulers** [שֹׁפְטֵינוּ, *šōpĕṭênû*—a form of שָׁפַט, *šāpaṭ*] who **ruled us** [שְׁפָטוּנוּ, *šĕpāṭûnû*—a form of שָׁפַט, *šāpaṭ*], by bringing upon us a great calamity." These verses demonstrate that שָׁפַט (*šāpaṭ*) is not limited to judicial contexts but can also be used to refer to various types of leadership. The fact that this range of meaning is not pointed out by EBC does not mean that the commentary author is unaware of the range of meaning; assume that a commentary's given meaning for a word applies (or is argued to apply) to the particular context under discussion, rather than to the word's every occurrence.

As for 2 Chronicles 1:10, we learned from CBC that Solomon first asks for wisdom and knowledge to *lead* the Israelites *in battle*; thus it makes good contextual sense for the parallel שָׁפַט (*šāpaṭ*) to mean *govern* or *lead* in a more general sense, in accord with ESV and NIV, rather than being limited to *rendering judgements*. Since Solomon did have a judicial role in Israel, this general leadership would include the rendering of judgements. It is also possible that שָׁפַט (*šāpaṭ*) includes *rendering judgements* in its meaning in 2 Chronicles 1:10. This possibility is supported by the fact that the parallel 1 Kings 3:9 is followed by the account of Solomon rendering a wise judgement in the case of the two prostitutes discussed earlier. It is possible for a word to convey more than one of its meanings in certain contexts, but this is rare.

New Testament (1 Timothy 6)[20]

Verses 2b-5[21]

Teach and urge these things. If anyone **teaches a different doctrine** [ἑτεροδιδασκαλεῖ, *heterodidaskalei*] and does not **agree with** [προσέρχεται, *proserchetai*] the **sound** [ὑγιαίνουσιν, *hygiainousin*] **words** [λόγοις, *logois*] of our Lord Jesus Christ and the teaching that accords with godliness, he is puffed up with conceit and understands nothing. He has an unhealthy craving for controversy and for quarrels about words, which produce envy, dissension, **slander** [βλασφημίαι, *blasphēmiai*], evil suspicions, and constant friction among people who are depraved in mind and deprived of the truth, imagining that godliness is a means of gain.

ἑτεροδιδασκαλεῖ (*heterodidaskalei*—a form of ἑτεροδιδασκαλέω, *heterodidaskaleō*)

CBC (111)—"*Some people may contradict our teaching.* Lit., 'If someone [*tis*...][22] teaches different things' (*heterodidaskalei*...)."

Here is a Greek example of the use of "literally" in commentaries. In this case, "literally" is being used to indicate that ἑτεροδιδασκαλέω (*heterodidaskaleō*) is a compound word (other/different + to teach). As has already been pointed out, without a knowledge of Greek (or Hebrew or Aramaic for the Old Testament) that allows you to understand what is meant

---

[20]   The three NT commentaries used in this section are CBC (2009), EBC (2006), and NIVAC (1999).

[21]   Bolded words indicate which words are used in the ESV to translate the Greek words that are discussed below.

[22]   Brackets are original.

by any particular use of "literally" in a commentary, simply gloss over the information there. It will only mislead you into thinking that a "literal" meaning is what the text *really* means.

EBC (552)—"**3-5** These verses hark back to Paul's opening remarks in 1:3-4 (note *heterodidaskaleō*..., 'teach false doctrines,' in 1:3 and 6:3)."

Turning to the comments on 1:3 (p 500) we read,

> The term 'teach false doctrines' is one word in the original (*heterodidaskalein*...) and may be a Pauline coinage. ...At least since Paul charged the Judaizers with preaching a 'different gospel' (*heteron euangelion*; Gal 1:6), the apostle displayed a concern that the one true gospel be preserved pure and free from accretions that emptied it of its saving power (cf. Ro 1:16-17).

The comments here in EBC can be used with much profit. In the comments on p 552, the only information given about ἑτεροδιδασκαλέω (*heterodidaskaleō*) is an English rendering, "teach false doctrines." When you come across such English renderings of biblical words, the commentator is giving you the English so that you know what word is being discussed, not to give you any definitive meaning of the word. For this reason, it is common to find in commentaries a biblical word, an English rendering of that word (often based on the translation used in the commentary, as is the case here with EBC), and then an argument for the meaning of the word that contradicts the rendering already given. Use the renderings of biblical words, such as "teach false doctrines" above, to follow the argument of the commentator, not to draw any implications about the meaning of the word.

The comments then on p 500 begin with the helpful note that ἑτεροδιδασκαλέω (*heterodidaskaleō*) "may be a Pauline coinage." This is helpful because it lets you know that the word only occurs in Pauline writings, and if such a compound word is a Pauline coinage (remember, only a *possibility*), then its meaning will most likely reflect the meanings of its component parts (in this case, "to teach something different"), since Paul would certainly expect his readers to understand the meaning of his newly-coined word without him there to define it. The remainder of the EBC quotation does not relate to the meaning of ἑτεροδιδασκαλέω (*heterodidaskaleō*) but does let you know that the concern for true teaching about Jesus, so evident in 1 Timothy, can also be found in other Pauline writings.

NIVAC (203)—"The verb for teaching false doctrines (*heterodidaskaleo*) appeared in 1:3 (see comments)."

The comments at 1:3 (p 53) read,

> The word translated 'teach false doctrines' (*heterodidaskaleo*) reappears in 6:3. That context shows that it is not merely something 'different' (as in the NRSV), as the etymology of this word ('teach [something][23] different') might by itself imply. Since in chapter 6 this verb is set in contrast to 'the sound instruction of our Lord Jesus Christ' and to 'godly teaching,' we know that what is not 'sound' is not only different; it is false. In Galatians 1:6-8 Paul says that the 'different gospel' that people were turning to was 'really no gospel at all' and that anyone who preached another 'gospel' should be 'eternally condemned.' To weaken

---

[23] Brackets are original.

heterodidaskaleo is to undervalue Paul's strong
teachings about truth and error.

The comments on ἑτεροδιδασκαλέω (*heterodidaskaleō*)
in NIVAC at 1 Timothy 6:3 are similar to those of EBC, start-
ing with an NIV-based English rendering of the verb, and then
directing the reader's attention to further discussion of the
word at 1:3. The longer quotation begins with a good recogni-
tion that a word's etymology is not a definite indicator of its
meaning, and so the fallacy of *Time Warp* is commendably
avoided. However, this quotation serves as a good example of
something that you will regularly find in commentaries: discussion about a word that initially takes into account how
words work and avoids word-study fallacies, but by the end of
the discussion is not so good.

The comments at first progress well, noting to what
ἑτεροδιδασκαλέω (*heterodidaskaleō*) is contextually contras-
ted, and rightly concluding that this different teaching is not
just different, but false. Then Galatians 1:6-8 is mentioned, as
it was in EBC, in which Paul clearly states the unpleasant
eternal destiny of those who preach a different gospel. Unfor-
tunately, NIVAC makes it clear that this information is
perceived as significant for the *meaning* of ἑτεροδιδασκαλέω
(*heterodidaskaleō*), when in the last sentence of the above
quotation, NIVAC writes, "To weaken *heterodidaskaleo* is to
undervalue Paul's strong teachings about truth and error."
Based upon what is written in NIVAC, a so-called "weakened"
meaning of ἑτεροδιδασκαλέω (*heterodidaskaleō*) would be
something like "to teach something different" rather than the
implied necessary meaning of the word, "to teach something
false."

There are a couple of reasons why NIVAC has gone
astray in concluding that ἑτεροδιδασκαλέω (*heterodi-*

daskaleō) *must* mean "to teach something false." First, remember that EBC mentioned the possibility that this word was coined by Paul, and remember that I said that if Paul coined this word, then it likely retains the meanings of its component parts. This first point at least means that "to teach something different" is a possible meaning for ἑτεροδιδασκαλέω (*heterodidaskaleō*). Second, NIVAC has subtly skewed the evidence in favour of the meaning, "to teach something false." This skewing of evidence started by noting that contextually in 1 Timothy 6, this teaching is false, and then progressed by noting that the "different gospel" in Galatians 1:6-8 was false. This use of Galatians 1:6-8 is problematic first of all because "different gospel" in Galatians 1:6 is not the word ἑτεροδιδασκαλέω (*heterodidaskaleō*) but two words: ἕτερον εὐαγγέλιον (*heteron euangelion*), as was noted above in EBC. Therefore, what NIVAC has done is taken information from the context of 1 Timothy 6 and information from Galatians 1:6-8 (where ἑτεροδιδασκαλέω [*heterodidaskaleō*] does not even occur!) and applied this information to the meaning of ἑτεροδιδασκαλέω (*heterodidaskaleō*), which is *Swamp Water*. Thus NIVAC's reasons for translating ἑτεροδιδασκαλέω (*heterodidaskaleō*) as "to teach something false" are not compelling.

Admittedly, many who read this book will not have enough knowledge of Greek to sift through NIVAC's comments in the way that I have here. So how would you respond to the comment that a "weakened" meaning of ἑτεροδιδασκαλέω (*heterodidaskaleō*), something like "to teach something different," "is to undervalue Paul's strong teachings about truth and error"? First, the fact that "teaches different things" is given as the meaning of the verb in CBC, similarly translated in the ESV, and similarly given as the etymology of the word in NIVAC, should caution you from discarding this meaning of the verb outright. Second, the possibility that Paul may have coined the term (suggested in EBC) should cause you to consider more seriously the possibility that the verb may mean something like "to teach something different." Third, if you read 1 Timothy in the ESV, which "weakly" translates the verb "teaches a different doctrine," and follow Paul's argument carefully, you will be able to realize that, as NIVAC says, "we know that what is not 'sound' is not only different; it is false." Therefore, Paul can be understood correctly whether ἑτεροδιδασκαλέω (heterodidaskaleō) is translated "to teach something different" or "to teach something false." In neither case are "Paul's strong teachings about truth and error" necessarily undervalued.

If Paul can be understood correctly with either of the above translations, then you may be wondering why it is important to note the error in what NIVAC has written. First, when our goal is to understand the Scriptures, we need to recognize the possibility that any misunderstanding of the text might lead to a skewed view of God or a false application of the text to our lives, no matter how minor a misunderstanding of the text might appear to be. Second, seeing "to teach something different" as a weakened and flawed understanding of ἑτεροδιδασκαλέω (heterodidaskaleō) can lead to the danger of drawing theology from words rather than sentences and paragraphs, a danger that this book is trying to help you avoid. The possibility that ἑτεροδιδασκαλέω (heterodidaskaleō) means "to teach something different" can help you recognize the fact that Paul presents his own teaching as the standard to which other teachings are to be compared for similarity or difference, and thereby truth or error. In 1 Timothy 6:2b, Paul tells Timothy to "Teach and urge these things," with "these things" being the things that Paul has taught previously in his letter. Then Paul criticizes those who teach "other things," that is, things that differ from what Paul teaches. This connection in what Paul says certainly can be noticed with a translation of "to teach something false" for ἑτεροδιδασκαλέω (*heterodi-daskaleō*) in 1 Timothy 6:3, but the connection is more likely to be missed by you if you flat out reject the *possibility* that the verb may be appropriately translated as "to teach something different."

προσέρχεται (*proserchetai*—a form of προσέρχομαι, *proserchomai*)

EBC (552)—"The term *proserchomai* (… only here in the PE [Pastoral Epistles]) here has the specialized sense 'agree with' or 'accede to'."

CBC (112)—"***but these are***. The Greek clause is *kai mē proserchetai* … (adhere), meaning 'and does not adhere to.' To adhere to something is to mentally agree with it."

In most of its New Testament occurrences the meaning of the compound word προσέρχομαι (*proserchomai*) reflects the meanings of its component parts (toward + come), such as in Matthew 4:11, "Then the devil left him, and behold, angels **came** [προσῆλθον, *proselthon*] and were ministering to him." For this reason, EBC is helpful when it says that the word in 1 Timothy 6:3 "here has the specialized sense 'agree with' or 'accede to'," indicating that the word does not always have this meaning. The range of meaning of the word προσέρχομαι (*proserchomai*) allows it to be used in contexts such as Matthew 4:11 to describe angels "coming to" Jesus, as well as in contexts such as 1 Timothy 6:3, where Timothy is warned about those who do not "agree with" sound doctrine. Notice that the meaning of προσέρχομαι (*proserchomai*) in 1 Timothy 6:3 is given in similar terms in both the EBC and CBC commentaries, but CBC does not state that the meaning given ("adhere") is the word's meaning in *this* context, rather than in all of its occurrences. As a general rule, when a commentary gives you the meaning of a word, assume that the given meaning applies to that particular context rather than to the word in its every occurrence.

It is important to notice that in both EBC and CBC, the "meaning" of προσέρχομαι (*proserchomai*) is simply given in English words: *agree with, accede to*, and *adhere to*. Since English and Greek are different languages, προσέρχομαι (*proserchomai*) does not actually mean *agree with, accede to*, or *adhere to*. These are not definitions but English words that can be used to translate προσέρχομαι (*proserchomai*) in 1 Timothy 6:3. For this reason, much caution is needed when encountering these types of statements in commentaries. It is easy to assume that the connotations that come to mind with *agree with* or *accede to*, for example, are connotations that are also true of προσέρχομαι (*proserchomai*), but this may or may not be true. For example, one might conclude that *accede to* suggests a person who at one time disagreed with "the sound words of our Lord Jesus Christ" but has now come to believe them. On the other hand, one could draw from *adhere to* the inference that Paul is referring to people who both mentally agree with and physically obey "the sound words of our Lord Jesus Christ." Indeed, a common tendency is to take these inferences that come to mind from *accede to* in EBC and *adhere to* in CBC, add them together, and conclude that προσέρχομαι (*proserchomai*) means "to mentally agree with something that at one time was not believed, and to physically obey it." This would, however, be an instance of the *Swamp Water* fallacy.

A knowledge of Greek that allows you to examine an entire biblical passage in Greek, including the way in which προσέρχομαι (*proserchomai*) is connected with other words, would be necessary to know whether the connotations that come to your mind with phrases such as *agree with, accede to,* or *adhere to* are connotations that are true of the word προσέρχομαι (*proserchomai*) in 1 Timothy 6:3. Without such knowledge of Greek, it is impossible to know if connotations derived from English words are true of the Greek word in question. We are, then, left with our English Bibles. The ESV of 1 Timothy 6:3 reads in part, "If anyone teaches a different doctrine and does not agree with the sound words of our Lord Jesus Christ ...." The rendering of this translation accords with what is written in CBC, "To adhere to something is to mentally agree with it." It is "the sound words of our Lord Jesus Christ" that Paul says need to be mentally agreed with, or believed. As we know from EBC, this meaning is true of the word in this verse, but not necessarily everywhere it occurs. Therefore, the information found in EBC and CBC regarding προσέρχομαι (*proserchomai*) lines up with what we would likely conclude about "not agree with" when reading 1 Timothy 6:3 in our English Bibles, but does not increase our understanding of the passage.

ὑγιαίνουσιν (*hygiainousin*—a form of ὑγιαίνω, *hygiainō*)

EBC (552)—" 'Sound' (*hygiainō*, ...) relates both to the character of the instruction and to its effects in the lives of those who heed it."

Statements such as this should raise a warning flag in your mind. When 1 Timothy 6:3 is read in English, it seems that it is specifically and only the "words of our Lord Jesus Christ" that are said to be "sound." This fact could easily lead you to believe that EBC is saying that the word ὑγιαίνω (*hygiainō*) contains within itself a double reference: to instruction *and* to the lives of those who heed such instruction. Such a belief could lead to an understanding of 1 Timothy 6:3-5 that people who both (i) do not mentally agree with sound instruction, and also (ii) do not live sound lives, are "puffed up with conceit" and exhibit the disruptive behaviour described by Paul in those verses. This would not be too surprising, since disruptive behaviour would naturally not be characteristic of those living "sound lives." So where is the problem?

The problem with the double-reference view of ὑγιαίνω (hygiainō) is that it is incorrect and actually disrupts Paul's argument. It is only the "words of our Lord Jesus Christ" that are described as "sound," a fact that is easily discerned from the English of 1 Timothy 6:3. The significance of this is that Paul, throughout 1 Timothy, including 6:3-5, shows the strong connection between belief and action: right belief leads to right action and wrong belief leads to wrong action. Paul is saying that those who reject "the sound words of our Lord Jesus" end up living destructive lives. The order that Paul gives —wrong belief leads to wrong action—is disrupted when "sound" is taken to refer to both the instruction and people's lives. Is the point then that wrong belief and wrong actions can be seen in certain specific wrong actions? Such a "disrupted view" might lead someone to conclude that wrong belief is not so bad, but that it is really wrong belief and wrong action in combination that is the problem. This conclusion is completely contrary to Paul's argument.

Without the ability to examine the use of ὑγιαίνω (hygiainō) in the New Testament and how it is connected with the other Greek words in 1 Timothy 6:3, you cannot verify or reject what EBC says about the word. However, when a statement in a commentary about a biblical word seems to suggest that it contains a double-reference within itself, as a general rule you should reject what the commentary says (since it smacks of *Swamp Water*) and stick with what you can infer from a reading of your English Bible. Doing so with ὑγιαίνω (*hygiainō*) in 6:3 would lead to the correct understanding that our beliefs impact our actions.

NIVAC (203)—"The word 'sound' represents the participle of the verb *hygiaino*, conveying the idea of being in good health (see comments on 1:10)." There is a footnote here that reads, "See also 2 Tim. 1:13; 4:3; Titus 1:9, 13; 2:1."

The much lengthier comment on 1:10 (p 65) reads,

> The expression 'sound teaching' occurs only in the Pastoral Letters. 'Sound' represents the participle of the verb *hygiaino*, 'to be healthy,' used as an adjective [a footnote here reads: 'Occurrences of the verb in the Pastoral Letters in addition to 1:10 are 6:3; 2 Tim. 1:13; 4:3; Titus 1:9, 13; 2:1-2.']. It is combined with 'words,' 'doctrine,' or 'in the faith.' In each case, it is used to describe true belief. Usually the immediate context shows that it is true belief in contrast to false teaching. The verb alone, in its literal sense of being healthy, is found elsewhere in the New Testament only in Luke and 3 John.
>
> This is a vivid figurative expression, specially employed in the Pastoral Letters to describe teaching that is not 'sick,' but wholesome and resistant to the disease of error. The false teachers, by contrast, had an 'unhealthy [*nosos*, sick][24] interest' in quarrels (1 Tim. 6:4). The sins that counter the Ten Commandments, listed in 1:9-10, are 'contrary to' this sound doctrine.

---

[24] These brackets are original.

There is a lot of information about ὑγιαίνω (hygiainō) here in NIVAC, and it is easy to get lost in the details.[25] The potential dangers begin on p 203 where it is written that ὑγιαίνω (hygiainō) conveys "the idea of being in good health." Similarly, on p 65 ὑγιαίνω (hygiainō) is said to mean "to be healthy," and we are told that the word is used "in its literal sense of being healthy" in Luke and 3 John. The danger with these statements is that you might be tempted to think that "to be physically healthy" is what ὑγιαίνω (hygiainō) *really* means, as can be seen in a verse like Luke 5:31, "And Jesus answered them, '**Those who are well** [ὑγιαίνοντες, *hygiainontes*—a form of ὑγιαίνω, *hygiainō*] have no need of a physician, but those who are sick....' " Remember, though, that each word has a range of meaning, so to demand that each word *really* means one thing that can be seen in its every occurrence is to commit the fallacy of *All Meanings Lead to Rome*.

It is, of course, possible that a word will be used in the New Testament every time with the same meaning, but this needs to be demonstrated rather than assumed to be true. Without a knowledge of Greek that allows you to examine every use of ὑγιαίνω (hygiainō) in the New Testament, you cannot know for sure if it is always used with the same meaning, like "to be physically healthy," or not. However, there are a couple of things you can notice in NIVAC that should cause you to question the idea that ὑγιαίνω (hygiainō) has one meaning that is always evident in the New Testament.

First, the NIV (used in NIVAC) translates ὑγιαίνω (hygiainō) with "sound," which would seem to suggest

---

[25]   The footnote at 1 Timothy 1:10 (p 65) has the correct listing of every occurrence of ὑγιαίνω (hygiainō) in the Pastoral Letters, with Titus 2:2 mistakenly left out of the footnote on p 203. Minor mistakes like this are commonly made in commentaries, so do not trust the given references for any biblical word.

instruction that is free from error rather than free from disease or sickness. Second, NIVAC says that ὑγιαίνω (*hygiainō*) is usually used for "true belief in contrast to false teaching." This statement again suggests a meaning for ὑγιαίνω (*hygiainō*) more along the lines of "free from error" rather than "physically healthy." These two factors, along with the fact that words have a range of meaning, should lead you to the conclusion that ὑγιαίνω (*hygiainō*) can be used in certain contexts to describe people who are physically healthy (e.g. Luke 5:31), but in other contexts (e.g. 1 Tim 6:3) to describe things that are free from error or correct.

A thought that may have passed through your mind is the possibility that ὑγιαίνω (*hygiainō*) is used in 1 Timothy 6:3 to describe instruction that is free from error, through the use of a metaphor. That is, perhaps this instruction is metaphorically described as healthy, which we understand to mean that it is free from error. This is, in fact, the argument of EBC, found at 1:10 (p 505),

> The term 'sound' (ὑγιαίνω, *hygiainō*...) constitutes a medical metaphor referring to the 'healthy' nature of teaching found in the gospel (v. 11) in contrast to the false teachers' 'unhealthy' interest (6:4) in strange doctrines that will 'spread like gangrene' (2 Ti 2:17; similar to cancer). The metaphor is not found earlier in Paul.

Although the use of a metaphor here is possible, one cannot assume that it is a metaphor, even though Paul does use medical imagery throughout the Pastoral Letters (See 1 Tim 6:4; 2 Tim 2:17; this is all that EBC's reference to these verses demonstrate. The fact that medical imagery is found in the Pastoral Letters certainly points to the possibility that ὑγιαίνω [*hygiainō*] is used metaphorically in 6:3, but it does not demonstrate this). If I were to see someone adding to a glass of iced tea a random assortment of ingredients, such as prunes, brown sugar, vanilla, cabbage, ketchup, oatmeal, and mayonnaise, I might look at the person's glass and say, "That is sick." In saying, "that is sick," I would simply mean that the glass's contents look and likely taste disgusting, rather than metaphorically being diseased and unhealthy. It is tempting, particularly for the sake of a sermon illustration, to find metaphorical uses of words in every passage of Scripture, but the use of a metaphor needs to be demonstrated rather than assumed to be true. Otherwise we may be emphasizing something that was never intended to be emphasized.

Like EBC, NIVAC makes much of "healthy" connotations for ὑγιαίνω (hygiainō) in 1 Timothy 6:3, partially based upon the fact that the "false teachers, by contrast, had an 'unhealthy [nosos, sick][26] interest' in quarrels (1 Tim. 6:4)." At first glance, the use of "unhealthy" to describe the false teachers seems to support a metaphorical understanding of "healthy" for ὑγιαίνω (hygiainō) in verse 3. However, do not forget the reasons already given for why ὑγιαίνω (hygiainō) should be taken here to mean something like *correct*. The fact that Paul describes these false teachers in verse 4 as having an "unhealthy craving for controversy" is probably a word-play that picks up on the fact that ὑγιαίνω (hygiainō) can be used to describe healthy people. This word-play does not change the meaning of ὑγιαίνω (hygiainō) in verse 3 from *correct* or *sound* to *healthy*, but it does draw a more explicit contrast between the teaching that should be accepted and the teachers whose teaching should be rejected.

CBC (112)—"*the wholesome teachings*. This is a phrase that is unique to the Pastorals (cf. 1:10; 2 Tim 4:3; Titus 1:9; 2:1)"; (114)—"To be 'wholesome' is to be healthy and correct.

---

[26] Brackets are original.

Paul gave 'wholesome teaching' and spoke what is 'right' (1:10; 6:3; 2 Tim 4:3; Titus 1:9; 2:1). The pattern of wholesome teaching is one Timothy himself was encouraged to follow (2 Tim 1:13). Titus was instructed to rebuke the false teachers so that they would become 'wholesome' in their faith (Titus 1:13; NLT, 'strong'). He was also to encourage older men to be 'wholesome' in faith (Titus 2:2; NLT, 'sound') and to be a model himself of correct speech (Titus 2:7-8). Wholesome teaching is correct because it is 'of our Lord Jesus Christ' (not a diseased mind) and craves 'the truth' (not controversy; 6:3, 5)."

CBC's discussion of ὑγιαίνω (hygiainō) shares many similarities with NIVAC; those similarities will not be re-discussed here, but there are two additional things to notice. The longer quotation (p 114) begins with a statement that adds together the two different meanings that have been suggested for the verb: *healthy* and *correct*. This is an instance of *Swamp Water*, which appears to be a result of the fact that ὑγιαίνω (hygiainō) is used in the New Testament to mean *healthy*, and because this "healthy instruction" in 1 Timothy 6 is correct. Remember that each word has a range of meaning, but the meaning of a word in a particular context usually only reflects part of that range of meaning. If you are able to recognize this occurrence of *Swamp Water* in CBC, you will not be led astray by what is written there, but there is a second problem with the above quotation. The way it is worded makes it appear that ὑγιαίνω (hygiainō) is used in Titus 2:7-8, but this is not actually the case. Rather, the cognate word ὑγιής (hygiēs) appears in verse 8, something that requires a knowledge of Greek to discover (and so Greek is worth learning!). The reference to Titus 2:7-8 is helpful for showing the importance of sound doctrine throughout the Pastoral Letters, but it is not helpful for determining the meaning of ὑγιαίνω (hygiainō) in 1 Timothy 6:3. Carefully think through what you are reading in commentaries since it is often difficult to discern if a comment is intended to apply to the meaning of a word or to a larger theme. If uncertain, assume that it applies to the larger theme.

λόγοις (*logois*—a form of λόγος, *logos*)

NIVAC (203) —"The NIV 'instruction' represents the plural of *logos*, which has a broader meaning than just 'words.' Thus, it need not refer to the specific words of Christ, though it is sometimes taken to do so (as in NRSV). The Pastorals do not cite specific quotations of Christ that the heretics contradict. Rather, their teaching is against the basic doctrines that he taught his followers."

The ESV also uses "words" to translate λόγοις (*logois*) in 6:3; since "words" is the most commonly used English word to translate λόγοις (*logois*), NIVAC is making an argument for why the NIV's "instruction" is a legitimate translation in this context. Since, according to NIVAC, the false teachers teach against doctrines rather than specific words or quotations of Jesus, the NIV's translation is perfectly acceptable. Therefore, although at first glance, NIVAC's statement that λόγος (*logos*) "has a broader meaning than just 'words'" might appear like *Swamp Water*, suggesting that λόγος (*logos*) means "words" and more, this is not the case. Instead, it is being argued that the range of meaning of λόγος (*logos*) allows it to be used for individual words, but also for instruction or doctrine that is composed of multiple words. For this reason, NIVAC's statement, when understood properly, is quite helpful for considering possible meanings of verse 3.

βλασφημίαι (*blasphēmiai*—a form of βλασφημία, *blasphēmia*)

CBC (112)—"*slander.* Lit., 'blasphemy.' This is not blasphemy against God but falsely maligning another believer's reputation (cf. Col 3:8)."

EBC (552)—"...'malicious talk' (*blasphēmiai*...; NASB, 'abusive language'; Mt 15:19; Mk 3:28; Jude 9);...'malicious talk' refers to speech..."

NIVAC (204)—"...'malicious talk' (*blasphemiai*, in this case slandering one another, not God)..."

The quotation from CBC is helpful to show the problematic nature of the word "literally" as it is used in commentaries. We are told by CBC that βλασφημίαι (*blasphēmiai*) is literally "blasphemy." The reason CBC says this is that *blasphemy* is the most commonly used English word to translate βλασφημία (*blasphēmia*), and the two words are in fact etymologically related. However, there are two problems with CBC's use of *literally*. First, the Greek word is plural, so *blasphemies* is more literal than *blasphemy*. Second, we usually use *blasphemy* in reference to things said about God or sacred things, rather than people, so it seems strange to be told that the Greek word is literally "blasphemy," but that it means "falsely maligning another believer's reputation" in this context. Aside from this comment, everything else said in the commentaries about βλασφημίαι (*blasphēmiai*) in verse 4 is in agreement with each other. The listed verses are other places where the Greek word βλασφημία (*blasphēmia*) occurs in the New Testament (although not all of its occurrences—never assume that this is the case).

EBC does give the NASB translation of "abusive language" for βλασφημίαι (*blasphēmiai*), which is not necessarily the same as "slander," although certainly encompasses slander. Remember what was discussed earlier, that connotations which come to mind with English words are not necessarily valid connotations for the Greek words that they translate. So do not press the meaning of either *slander* or *abusive language*. In either case, someone else is being maligned or verbally criticized; this is the key point that you should come away with from what is written in these commentaries.

CONCLUSION

Hebrew and Greek words are often spoken of as magnificent gems that contain within themselves great theological meaning simply waiting to be mined. The impression thus tends to be given that those who do not (or cannot) mine these magnificent gems are hopelessly lost with an inability to understand the Scriptures. At the end of this short book, you should be able to set aside this notion and instead recognize the simple, yet profound, reality that God has given us literature and not a dictionary. The Bible is a book filled with sentences and paragraphs rather than disconnected words. Thus our task is not to build theology on individual words but on what is conveyed through the sentences and paragraphs of Scripture.

As I hope you have picked up in the pages of this book, there is great value in learning the biblical languages, so I encourage you to learn them and enjoy the privilege of reading and studying God's Word in its original languages. In the meantime, evaluate statements you read about biblical words based on what you have learned in the pages of this book. In the process, may your understanding of the Scriptures grow and your love for the Lord increase abundantly.

BIBLIOGRAPHY

Arnold, Bill T. and H. G. M. Williamson, eds. 2005. *Dictionary of the Old Testament: Historical Books.* Downers Grove, IL: InterVarsity. S.v. "High Places," by Donna L. Petter.

Barr, James. 2004. *The Semantics of Biblical Language.* Oxford: Oxford University Press, 1961; reprint, Eugene, OR: Wipf & Stock (page references are to reprint edition).

Baxter, Benjamin J. 2009-10. The Meanings of Biblical Words. *McMaster Journal of Theology and Ministry* 11: 89-120.

_____. 2010-11. Hebrew and Greek Word-Study Fallacies. *McMaster Journal of Theology and Ministry* 12: 3-32.

Belleville, Linda. 2009. 1 Timothy. In *1 Timothy; 2 Timothy, Titus; Hebrews*, ed. Philip W. Comfort, 25-123. Cornerstone Biblical Commentary 17. Carol Stream, IL: Tyndale House.

Boda, Mark J. 2004. "Lexical Analysis." Class notes for Intermediate Hebrew I. Hamilton, ON: McMaster Divinity College.

_____. 2009. *A Severe Mercy: Sin and Its Remedy in the Old Testament.* Siphrut: Literature and Theology of the Hebrew Scriptures 1. Winona Lake, IN: Eisenbrauns.

_____. 2010. *1-2 Chronicles.* Cornerstone Biblical Commentary 5a. Carol Stream, IL: Tyndale House.

Carson, D. A. 1996. *Exegetical Fallacies*. 2d ed. Grand Rapids, MI: Baker.

_____. 2000. *The Difficult Doctrine of the Love of God*. Wheaton, IL: Crossway.

Crossway Bibles. 2001. *The Holy Bible: English Standard Version*. Wheaton, IL: Good News.

Encyclopædia Britannica. 2009 ed. S.v. "Dynamite." Accessed June 19, 2009. http://www.britannica.com/EBchecked/topic/175198/dynamite.

Groom, Susan Anne. 2003. *Linguistic Analysis of Biblical Hebrew*. Waynesboro, GA: Paternoster.

Hill, Andrew E. 2003. *1 & 2 Chronicles*. The NIV Application Commentary. Grand Rapids, MI: Zondervan.

Jenson, Philip. 1992. *Graded Holiness: A Key to the Priestly Conception of the World*. JSOTSup 106. Sheffield: JSOT Press.

Köstenberger, Andreas. 2006. 1 Timothy. In *Ephesians-Philemon*, ed. Tremper Longman III and David E. Garland, 487-561. The Expositor's Bible Commentary: Revised Edition 12. Grand Rapids, MI: Zondervan.

Liefeld, Walter L. 1999. *1 & 2 Timothy, Titus*. The NIV Application Commentary. Grand Rapids, MI: Zondervan.

Mabie, Frederick J. 2010. 1 and 2 Chronicles. In *1 Chronicles-Job*, ed. Tremper Longman III and David E. Garland, 23-336. The Expositor's Bible Commentary: Revised Edition 4. Grand Rapids, MI: Zondervan.

Merriam-Webster Online Dictionary. 2010 ed. S.v. "Nephew." Accessed January 14, 2010. http://www.merriam-webster.com/dictionary/nephew.

Oxford Dictionaries, April 2010a ed. S. v. "Bank." Accessed March 10, 2011. http://oxforddictionaries.com/definition/ bank?rskey=LGx6ex&result=1.

———. April 2010b ed. S. v. "Bank." Accessed March 17, 2011. http://oxforddictionaries.com/view/entry/m_en_gb 0059620?rskey=QduWEr&result=2.

———. April 2010c ed. S.v. "Gay." Accessed March 17, 2011. http://oxforddictionaries.com/view/entry/m_en_gb 0329310.

———. April 2010d ed. S.v. "Idiom." Accessed March 10, 2011. http://oxforddictionaries.com/view/entry/m_en_gb 0398660.

———. April 2010e ed. S.v. "Nice." Accessed March 18, 2011. http://oxforddictionaries.com/view/entry/m_en_gb 0557390?rskey=wRJCBm&result=2.

———. April 2010f ed. S.v. "Rapture." Accessed March 18, 2011. http://oxforddictionaries.com/definition/rapture? rskey=iblI6B&result=1.

———. April 2010g ed. S.v. "Synonym." Accessed March 17, 2011. http://oxforddictionaries.com/view/entry/m_en _gb0838680.

Silva, Moisés. 1983. *Biblical Words and Their Meaning: An Introduction to Lexical Semantics*. Grand Rapids: Zondervan.

Appendix A
TRANSLITERATION TABLES

Greek

Letter	Transliteration	Note
α	a	
β	b	
γ	g (n before γ, κ, ξ, and χ)	
δ	d	
ε	e	e as in bed
ζ	z	
η	ē	ay as in day
θ	th	
ι	i	i as in bit
κ	k	
λ	l	
μ	m	

Letter	Transliteration	Note
ν	n	
ξ	x	x as in box
ο	o	o as in box
π	p	
ρ	r	
σ, ς	s	
τ	t	
υ	Y (u in diphthongs)	u as in rude
φ	ph	
χ	ch	
ψ	ps	
ω	ō	o as in home
ῳ	ǭ	
ῃ	ḝ	
ᾳ	ą	
ʽ	*h (rough breathing)*	h as in home

Hebrew

Letter	Transliteration	Note
א	ʾ	not pronounced
ב	b	b/v
ג	g	
ד	d	d/th in these
ה	h	
ו	v	
ז	z	
ח	ḥ	ch as in loch
ט	ṭ	
י	y	
כ, ך	k	
ל	l	
מ, ם	m	
נ	n	
ס	s	
ע	ʿ	not pronounced

Letter	Transliteration	Note
פ, ף	p	p/f
צ, ץ	ṣ	ts
ק	q	
ר	r	
שׁ	š	sh
שׂ	ś	s
ת	t	t/th as in thin
בַ	a	a as in hat
בָ	ā	a as in father
בֶ	e	e as in bed
בֵ	ē, ê (with y)	ay as in bay
בִ	i, î (with y)	i as in bit, with y as in machine
בֹ	ō, ô (with silent v)	o as it vote
בֻ	u	u as in bull
ו	ū, û (with silent v)	u as in flute
בְ	ĕ	very short sound, similar to a in about

Letters with or without dagesh are not distinguished.

Vowel sounds not actually included in this book are not included in the table.

SCRIPTURE INDEX

Old Testament

New Testament

Also in the
Areopagus Critical Christian Issues Series

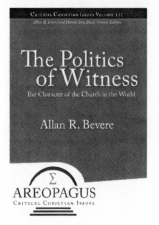

In *The Politics of Witness*, Dr. Allan R. Bevere asks why the church can't speak the truth effectively to power and proposes an answer. The church has come to depend too much on temporal power and has thus forgotten its divine authority. In finding this answer he goes back to the founding of the church and how it first became dependent on the state. He examines those who have followed, mostly building a political theory that takes the responsibility of ministry from the church and gives it to the state.

You'll find some names in this that might surprise you. Any discussion of Christianity and the state will involve Emperor Constantine, but what about his modern lieutenants, such as Locke, Jefferson, Franklin, and others?

While the theology applies to the church in any country, Dr. Bevere takes a particular look at the peculiarly American view that the United States of America is somehow God's chosen people, a nation of destiny in accomplishing the gospel mission.

Coming Soon!

"There is little in life so scintillating as a brief book with pungent, exciting, thought-provoking content. Ant Greenham in The Questioning God has achieved that goal with remarkable succinctness. For example, I learned more about Islam in chapters 3 and 4 than in all the rest of my reading on the subject in the last five years. Don't miss this prescient monograph."

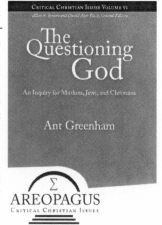

Paige Patterson
President
Southwestern Baptist Theological Seminary
Fort Worth, TX

More from Energion Publications

Personal Study

The Jesus Paradigm	$17.99
Finding My Way in Christianity	$16.99
When People Speak for God	$17.99
Holy Smoke, Unholy Fire	$14.99
Not Ashamed of the Gospel	$12.99
Evidence for the Bible	$16.99
Christianity and Secularism	$16.99
What's In A Version?	$12.99
Christian Archy	$9.99
The Messiah and His Kingdom to Come	$19.99 (B&W)

Christian Living

52 Weeks of Ordinary People – Extraordinary God	$7.99
Daily Devotions of Ordinary People – Extraordinary God	$19.99
Directed Paths	$7.99
Grief: Finding the Candle of Light	$8.99
I Want to Pray	$7.99
Soup Kitchen for the Soul	$12.99
The Sacred Journey	$11.99

Bible Study

Learning and Living Scripture	$12.99
To the Hebrews: A Participatory Study Guide	$9.99
Revelation: A Participatory Study Guide	$9.99
Ephesians: A Participatory Study Guide	$9.99
Philippians: A Participatory Study Guide	$9.99
The Gospel According to St. Luke: A Participatory Study Guide	$8.99
Identifying Your Gifts and Service: Small Group Edition	$12.99
Why Four Gospels?	$11.99

Theology

God's Desire for the Nations	$18.99
From Inspiration to Understanding	$24.99

Fiction

Megabelt	$12.99
Stories of the Way	$9.99

Energion Publications - P.O. Box 841
Gonzalez, FL 32560
Website: http://energionpubs.com
Phone: (850) 525-3916

CPSIA information can be obtained at www.ICGtesting.com
Printed in the USA
LVOW072009040212

267093LV00001B/87/P